# SPEED SECRETS 3

## INNER SPEED SECRETS

### MENTAL STRATEGIES TO MAXIMIZE YOUR RACING PERFORMANCE

**ROSS BENTLEY**
**RONN LANGFORD**

**MOTORBOOKS**
INTERNATIONAL

First published in 2000 by Motorbooks International, an imprint of MBI Publishing Company, Galtier Plaza, Suite 200, 380 Jackson Street, St. Paul, MN 55101-3885 USA

Motorbooks International titles are also available at discounts in bulk quantity for industrial or sales-promotional use. For details write to Special Sales Manager at Motorbooks International Wholesalers & Distributors, Galtier Plaza, Suite 200, 380 Jackson Street, St. Paul, MN 55101-3885 USA.

ISBN 0-7603-0834-9

Printed in the United States of America

# Contents

# *Acknowledgments*

First of all, I would like to once again thank everyone whom I acknowledged in my first book, *Speed Secrets*. Your input, motivation and support were the keys to that book, which obviously has led to this one. Of course, thank you to everyone who made *Speed Secrets* a success by purchasing it.

I really want to thank Ronn Langford, my mental coach and coauthor, for setting me on a path that has developed my abilities as a race driver and coach better than I ever would have without him. What I've learned in working with Ronn through the years, and particularly on this book, will help me throughout the rest of my life.

Thank you to everyone who helped in the development of this book—all those people who took the time to proofread, edit, provide feedback, and give encouragement. Also, to MBI Publishing, thank you for taking on both this book and *Speed Secrets*.

While doing research for this book, and for my own interest, I have read many books on subjects related to what Ronn and I discuss here. Most of them are listed in the Recommended Reading list in Appendix C. I would like to thank the authors of those books—they have helped me learn a lot.

Over the past few years, I've had the opportunity to work very closely with a number of race drivers. In providing personal coaching, I've been able to use them as test subjects for all the strategies presented in this book. I specifically want to thank Bob, Chris, Tim, Ryan, Jeffrey, and Lee for their openness and willingness to strive to be even better race drivers. I'm sure they didn't mind being my guinea pigs, as I imagine they enjoyed the improvements they made as much as I did.

Next to what I've learned about applying *Inner Speed Secrets* from coaching race drivers, I've learned almost as much from my daughter, Michelle. I dedicate this book to her, and hope she enjoys her personal performance in whatever endeavors she chooses throughout her life as much as I will enjoy observing her.

And finally, thanks again to my wife, Robin, for all her support, assistance, and dedication.

—*Ross Bentley*

For several years, I have wanted to put all of the concepts that I have been privileged to learn and work with into a book. But when you're really focused upon your life purpose, it's easy to just put it on a back burner. So for several years, I worked on parts and pieces of this book and conducted some high-performance seminars just for the fun of it.

Then last year, Ross, who had just completed his book *Speed Secrets*, asked me about writing a book together, and calling it *Inner Speed Secrets*. It would be about the concepts that Ross and I have taught and worked with for many years, and, from Ross' perspective, how to implement the concepts at the highest potential level. Ross has done this over the past several years, and is experientially knowledgeable about the concepts.

We outlined the book and submitted it for consideration for publication. And sure enough, there was interest. So, I would first like to acknowledge Ross and his commitment to kicking me in the rear and getting the job done. Otherwise, it would never have been finished.

In addition, there are many others who have been my teachers and mentors over the years, far too many to name. Some of you know who you are—for others, we'll talk about it in the future. I would like to acknowledge specifically some who have taught me so much—Anthony Robbins, Dr. Paul Dennison, and Dr. Carla Hannaford.

Most of all, I would like to acknowledge the people I have been given the opportunity to work with, who have taught me more than all others combined. Gabe, Toni, Rita, Wes, and other clients who have had serious traumatic brain injuries and other debilitating conditions—they have taught me so much about what human potential really means, even after top neurologists had given up on them.

I would also like to dedicate this book to my daughter, Dorri. Dorri was a beautiful young woman, just graduated from high school and on her life path, when she was killed by a drunken driver. As a result, my personal mission was totally changed and my life was led into a unique and meaningful purpose.

And to Dani, my soul mate and life partner. You really complete me!

—*Ronn Langford*

# *Foreword*

Nearly everyone who has set foot to gas pedal has thought at some time that all he really needed to be up there with Fangio, Moss, Senna, and Schumacher, would be a really fast car, some practice, and a little luck. Indeed, those items are helpful, even necessary, but if you are making out a wish list to see you to a championship, don't put them at the top.

First, you'll need an appropriate physical and neurological make-up. Every endeavor requires a certain basic set of tools, both innate and learned. Michael Jordan's genetic code predisposed him to be a greater success playing above the rim than, say, riding Derby winners. Julia Child was similarly destined to be more successful with a bain-marie than a pas de deux. Like an uncarved block, you came into this world, potentialities to be realized (or not.)

The happenstances of your life and your environment roughed in the shape. You refined that with ever more precise tools. You watched. You did. You learned. Gradually, you formed from the formless. And now here you are. Interest, propensity, and circumstances have placed you on a starting grid, the shriek of engines dulled slightly by your earplugs. Your eyes are keen (or artfully corrected). Your heart rate is optimized by training and experience. You are ready for the flag to drop. What sets you apart from the others also waiting? You may differ in innate abilities. Some are more blessed than others. But you may differ more by how fully you have developed those abilities that are specific to this odd commotion of competing in a race car on a cast loop of roadway. And most important, because the differences are the greatest, where those tires nudge the staggered chalk lines, your ability is measured by how fully you have integrated your body, soul, and mind with a clarity of intent.

Truth be told, any fool can go fast. It takes something more to go very fast. To go faster still, to be among the fastest, takes the most careful burnishing of all that has come to you by nature and all that you have learned. Sometimes those endowed with all that nature can muster are able to coast on the early, easy successes of what they came with. To do well, they are not pressed to sharpen and particularize their talents. "Cursed with a flair," a friend of mine called it, as he looked back on the moments of flashy brilliance in an otherwise unrealized life. His successes came easily, so he was never moved to work for rewards beyond the immediate horizon. Probably you've known at least one driver who basked in early triumphs, whose natural talents later had the doors blown off by someone who cosseted a lesser legacy. He didn't know that the tortoise and the hare would be on the midterm.

It is now a sports cliché that the mental game is the real game. But clichés become clichés because of the truth within them. As you sit on that grid, as you fall in behind the pace car, your mind is the designated driver, whether you recognize it or not. It is best that it be well prepared. In 1975, when I wrote a book called *The Centered Skier*, my elevating the emotional and intellectual aspects of the sport to the same importance as the physical was dismissed as woo-woo stuff. When I taught guided fantasies and visualization, eyes rolled heavenward. So imagine my delight in finding that woo-woo stuff all these years later embraced as rock solid basics in Ronn and Ross' wonderful book. Hey, these guys get it! Furthermore, they have enlarged it and codified it. They can explain it and teach it, and they have made it practical, graspable, feasible, and readily available to you.

Just as with the secret of skiing, the great thing about the secret of speed is: It isn't secret! Had I gone on to write, say, *The Centered Driver*, I would hope that it would be *Inner Speed Secrets*. Welcome this book. Embrace it. Breathe it in and make it yours. Godspeed.

—*Denise McCluggage*

# Introduction

Do you want to maximize your performance as a race driver on a consistent basis? Do you want to understand how and why the superstars of the sport consistently perform at such a high level? What driver wouldn't?

If you are like most race drivers, there are some practice or qualifying sessions or races when everything goes just right, when you are magic in the car, when you're in the flow. And there are other times when nothing seems to go right, when you are decidedly not in the flow. Why is that? Why are there times in your job, your recreation or hobby, or your personal life, when everything you try works and other times when nothing works? Most of us remember some of these moments, but we have no idea why things happen the way they do.

Is it something you ate, something you were wearing, something you or someone else said? Is it physical? Is it the car? Or is it mental? Well, all of these things can play a role in how well you drive, but the prime overall factor determining your performance level in and out of the race car is mental. Unfortunately, most of us just don't have a very clear understanding of what *mental* means.

Professional athletes in many sports have been working with sports psychologists for several years. But only recently have race drivers begun to work on strategies for the mind. Visual processing skills, psychomotor response times, dynamic awareness, muscle response and control, and so on are finally being recognized as no less critical components than the engineering and set-up of a race car

Most race drivers and their teams, whether amateur or professional, spend the off season trying to get the race car more competitive—trying to develop more horsepower, trying to get better balance and handling, and trying to get the thing to stop. They spend serious dollars on developing the car, but they seldom spend anything on developing the driver.

Almost every type of automobile racing, with the possible exception of a few of the spec series, demands cubic dollars in order to be competitive. Formula One, Indy Cars, NASCAR, Le Mans/Prototypes, GT and Touring Cars, Indy Lights, Formula Atlantic, etc., have become bottomless pits into which international currencies are thrown. Even at the SCCA club racing level, as many dollars as one can afford (and sometimes more) are spent on the race car. And yet, most invest few dollars and little effort on the primary determinant of their performance and success—the primary management system of the race car, the driver. And the ultimate management system of the driver is, of course, the mind. When we talk, tongue-in-cheek, about the importance of the mental game, we really need to understand that the mind is the cause of our performance in a race car.

*All racing drivers at a certain level are given
a gift from God, a natural talent. The fellows
who are very good, and turn out to be
exceptional, exercise that talent to the fullest
extent through management of the mind.*

**—Jackie Stewart**

At times, most of us have experienced being "in the flow" or "in the zone." It is effortless. It is easy. It is a feeling of total connection. It is not accomplished by trying harder, or by willpower. In fact, for most of us this creates anxiety, and anxiety in any form slows down the mental processing within the brain and the communication to the rest of the body. It also creates immediate changes in body chemistry, which substantially inhibit our ability to access our skills.

Along with providing one-on-one race driver coaching, we conduct a seminar called *Inner Speed Secrets*. The seminar has been presented in two Sports Car Club of America National Conventions and dozens of cities throughout North America, and the concepts are now being used by race car drivers at all levels across the United States and Canada. Psychologists, psychiatrists, coaches, athletes, surgeons, nurses, parents, teachers, attorneys, all types of business people, and professional race drivers have participated in this seminar, and have been amazed at the results in their performance level behind the wheel of the race car, and in their personal and professional lives.

In addition to thousands of race drivers, we have had the opportunity to work with other athletes, including World Cup soccer players, Olympic-level cyclists, skiers, and others. We have also worked with many people who have had a traumatic brain injury, stroke, or other debilitating disease, as well as young people with various learning difficulties. We have gained a unique perspective and an opportunity to develop, experiment, and observe the effects of specific strategies. These are intended to increase an individual's performance level—especially in a highly competitive racing environment.

And most important, we have been able to hear about the results.

A few years ago, Ronn concluded a seminar at Sears Point with a one-and-one-half-hour track session. Fourteen participants, many of whom were running in professional series, cut at least a half-second off their personal-best lap time. A few even cut two seconds off—and this was on their home track! In addition, all drivers were able to identify a list of personal, specific objectives that they believed would help them increase their overall performance in the race car, and together they developed strategies for them to be able to make these changes. This included working on everything from concentration, focus, and consistency, to learning how to program better behavioral decisions and control emotions.

So, just how important is the mind in racing? In the past, most drivers used will power and wishful thinking, rather than realistic strategies with the objective of becoming an elite-level athlete. Race drivers have had a tendency to operate more on testosterone than on strategies. Then athletes such as Jack Nicklaus, Larry Bird, Bill Russell, Michael Jordan, Carl Lewis, Mike Powell, Ayrton Senna, Emerson Fittipaldi, and Michael Schumacher started implementing performance and superlearning strategies, using visualization techniques, and more. They started to learn how to develop the assets they already had.

Our goal here is to help you determine why you sometimes perform at your highest level, and what stops you from performing at your best. You can look at performance as if it were two sides of the same coin. On one side, what can I do to increase my performance level? On the other side, what can I not do that decreases my performance level? From there, it should be relatively simple to develop a strategy to enable you to perform consistently at your highest level.

Ultimately, we want to find the cause of good—even great—performance. If you can identify what causes great performance, then you can replicate that (i.e., what you can do that will induce "being in the zone"). And if you know what causes "bad" performance, you can make the necessary changes to avoid that.

# How This Book is Organized

Throughout this book we will suggest specific strategies (planned processes used to achieve a goal) that you can use to improve your performance behind the wheel of a race car. Without a strategy, you rarely make any constructive changes. This will include specific strategies for left/right brain integration, brain/body integration, visual integration, balance, mental preparation, building a belief system for the desired state of mind, at-track mental exercises, learning new techniques and tracks, and more. It will then be up to you to select the appropriate strategies and incorporate them into your own Personal Performance Plan.

We wanted the topics presented in this book to be easy to implement. After all, you can have all the information in the world, but if you don't do anything with it, your performance will never improve. For that reason, Appendix A is a very important part of *Inner Speed Secrets*. Appendix A is a list of all the specific strategies presented throughout the book. It is designed for you to pick and choose your very own Personal Performance Program—an overall program

*The real key to winning races is not the race car, but you, the driver. And the key to your performance—whether you win or lose—is your mind.*

consisting of all the strategies you decide to use. Of course, you will need to read the first 20 chapters to gain the full understanding, and therefore motivation, to implement these strategies.

We admit that you may feel a bit awkward or uncomfortable at first using some of the strategies we suggest here. Don't worry; you're not the only one. However, there are ways and places to do them where you won't feel that way. And, we're sure once you start performing at your very best on a consistent basis, everyone around you will want to know what your secret is. You can decide then if you want to show them your tools—your inner speed secrets.

Some of the strategies we suggest will not seem or feel *right* to you, while others will. Use the ones that feel right immediately, and try the others every now and then, and make note of the changes in your performance over time. Just because a strategy doesn't feel right or seem to be making a difference, doesn't mean you should dismiss it completely. The more strategies you use on a regular basis, the better a race driver you will be.

Although we will be looking at a variety of concepts and performance strategies separately, they are all interrelated. We can separate them into chapters for discussion purposes, but it is impossible to separate them functionally. By the end of the book we hope to tie everything together, and that it will all make sense to you.

We all know that one of the necessary ingredients for each of us to do anything is motivation. There are no quick, easy fixes. We do not have a pill that will quickly increase your performance level, nor a pill to give anyone motivation. Motivation is self-directed; it comes from your inner self making a decision to implement, to follow through, to work to change the way that you do things.

This requires a commitment. Motivation and commitment can be developed more easily when you believe that what you are doing will actually be effective. This belief, however, is subject to your understanding of the process. Without the understanding, few people will accept the strategies. That is why we will explain the why and how in this book. The better you understand the concepts, the stronger your belief in their effectiveness will be, and the stronger your motivation will be to use them.

Evidence of some success is also necessary to provide continued motivation. But without implementing these strategies, there can be no evidence. We have all heard people say "I tried that once, and it didn't work." And, "I knew it wouldn't work!" If you witnessed the success we've achieved with other race drivers— some of your competitors—you would have all the evidence and motivation you need. You may be able to argue about the theory of something, but when you see and experience the results, there is no argument. Once you begin to use these strategies, you will experience firsthand the results and gain all the motivation you need to continue.

By the way, throughout this book we will refer to the race driver as "he." This is in no way meant to imply women cannot drive race cars. It is used only for simplicity's sake. In fact, we often prefer coaching women, because they are usually more open to the learning process. Many men think they already know everything, at least about driving and maybe one other subject.

This book is meant to be a tool for successful race drivers. How would you feel if the mechanic preparing your race car learned all the most up-to-date technical performance-enhancing aspects of the car, bought all the latest tools and equipment, and then left them all back at the shop? It's exactly the same with this book—it is a tool. If you don't use it, it won't help you win more races. Simple as that. And trust us, many of your competitors are already using these tools.

,  And no matter how much natural talent you have, it is what you do with it—how you develop it, and how often you access it all—that will determine how successful you are. Your inner speed secrets determine your performance level, and therefore, how often you win.

*Somewhere, someone is practicing. And when you meet him in head to head competition, he will beat you!*

**—Anonymous**
(found on a wall at a canoe racing
club in Hilo, Hawaii)

*Throughout this book we will be throwing a lot of interrelated information at you all at once, hoping to tie it all together by the end. It's a lot like trying to juggle 19 balls all at once while talking about each one individually, and then catching them all at the same time.*

# Chapter 1

# *Performance*

Before we can get to what causes good and bad performance, we must first define and agree on exactly what performance is.

Western culture, and particularly competitive people like race drivers, usually define or rate performance by the outcome—the result. In other words, our perspective of performance is usually viewed in the past tense. We look at the effect rather than the cause. If you win, you tend to think of that as a great performance. If you lose, that is bad performance. But is that really what performance is all about? Is that the right way of looking at it? It is certainly one way, but we'd like to ask you to look at it differently.

Have you ever won a race after making a number of mistakes, knowing you could have done better? Was that a great performance? Have you ever finished 3rd, 5th, or even 10th, but felt you got everything possible out of your car on that day? Was that a bad performance? In other words, how many times have you per-

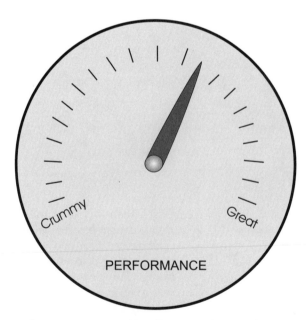

*Typically, your performance as a race driver lies somewhere on the spectrum between crummy and great. Wouldn't you prefer it to be great all the time?*

formed at your own personal maximum or best, and yet not had a *great* result, and vice versa?

By the pure definition of the word, shouldn't performance be related to how you performed, rather than on the result you achieved? We think so.

## INNER SPEED SECRET #1

### Focus on your performance, not the result.

We need to have a much better understanding of what causes performance—especially the performance of the driver. The performance spectrum ranges from crummy to great. We usually operate somewhere in between. From day to day, our performance level can change, although we usually have no idea why. If it's not because our skill changes from one day to the next, it must be something else. There are many potential reasons, which is why it can be so challenging to perform at a high level on a consistent basis.

### The Performance Model

Over the past several years, we have developed a model that we use with every program we teach. It allows us to look at performance differently, and attempt to understand what causes performance. We call it the Performance Model. Remember that we are using *performance* in terms of *cause*. Your time and your finishing position are the effect, or the result. Your performance is what caused the result. This model gives us a way to see, experience, and understand the cause of performance.

If we look at performance as a *cause*, then, and only then, can we define strategies. As an example, there are no cures for symptoms (effects), only remedies. We can give you two aspirin for a headache, and that may help with the symptom (pain). But it will not cure the cause of the headache.

If we can identify the cause, then we might be able to define a solution. If we can identify what causes you to perform at your highest level, we can develop a strategy. If we can identify what causes you to perform at your worst, we can develop strategies to avoid those causes.

First, we must understand the process. Then we can isolate specific personal (individual) objectives and define strategies for specific objectives.

We have all seen talented young drivers with the potential for reaching the elite level of motor racing, who were too aggressive, or had too little patience, were too rough on equipment, crashed too often, and never made it. People probably told them they were too aggressive, or needed more patience, or needed to save their car or tires, or crashed too often, and "not to do that." But it did no good! Why? Because it takes more than just saying "don't do that" to change a driver's mental programming. In other words, all they did was deal with the effect, not the cause.

This type of change does not occur as the result of a conscious level process or awareness. Let's assume that a driver has a reputation for having little patience and being too aggressive—the result being that hundreds of thousands of dollars of equipment has been destroyed. And so the team owner tells him again and again, "Don't do that!" Understand that a conscious level discussion, or specific instruction by a team owner or driving coach, does not change anything. Why? Because when a driver gets into the car, he is (or should be) driving at the subconscious level. Nothing has been done to change his subconscious programming. The net result will continue to be the same.

The Performance Model allows us to understand what causes performance. As we have said, we can look at performance as two sides of the same coin. First, what you can do to increase your performance level, and second, what you can not do that decreases your performance level. Most important, we will then define strategies that will help to make the necessary changes.

Your real goal is to get 100 percent out of yourself—to perform at your maximum level. To do that in auto racing, you must first separate yourself (perceptually) from the car, because as you know, your results are often dictated by the competitiveness of your car.

## INNER SPEED SECRET #2

### The goal is to get 100 percent out of yourself.

For the sake of our discussions let's place your race car's competitiveness on a performance scale of 0 to 100 percent. Then, grade your skill level on a scale of 0 to 100 percent. Understand that we are talking about your skill level as a race driver today. With more practice—concentrated, directed, effective practice—your skill level will improve. For example, if we use Michael Schumacher's skill level as a benchmark, setting it at 100, on the same scale yours may be 85 today. But with practice, over time, it may increase to 95, or even 100. (You might even reach 105 on Schumacher's scale, and when you do, we have a few team owners we'd like to introduce you to, and we'd like to be your agent!)

The race car and its systems are a critically important ingredient in the overall performance, but the car is capable of operating at the highest level only if the driver is up to it. That is, the car cannot make the driver outperform himself. Conversely, a driver cannot make a car outperform itself. And the driver cannot manage the car's systems until he learns to manage his own systems.

At the highest level of any sport, the differences between the best competitors are almost negligible. This is especially true in the race car, where a few hundredths of a second in each turn become the difference between a winner and an also-ran.

There is a lot of discussion regarding the allocation of importance of the car and driver, relative to each other. In a spec series (in which the cars are supposed to have as much similarity as possible), the driver is considered to make the difference. In CART Champ car racing today, there is a belief that the car is 80 to 90 percent of the performance envelope, with the driver being only 10 to 20 percent. Even the big-name drivers use this comparison.

We believe this discussion is inappropriate for the following reason. The car is what the car is. That is, you can work on developing horsepower, handling, aerodynamics, braking systems, and so on, and the driver is a very important part of that process. That is what testing programs are all about. But even a testing program is limited by the driver's ability to recognize, process, and store the dynamic changes in the car. Also, if we assume that the car is set at its maximum performance level, it is still only the driver that will make the car perform at that level.

For example, if you have 10 identical cars, with identical setup and identical engines, chassis and tires, what is the percentage of importance of the driver? Answer: 100 percent. If the cars are not identical, but you want to get 100 percent out of the car, what it the importance of the driver? One hundred percent again.

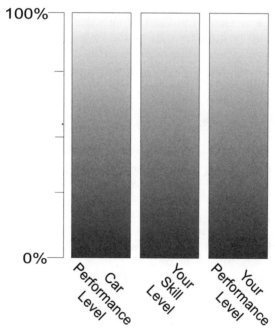

*Ultimately, your car's performance level and your own skill level will play a role in the results you achieve, but once you're behind the wheel the only thing you can control is your own performance level. Your goal should be to always perform at your best—your 100 percent.*

The driver is the most important ingredient! And getting the driver to a higher level of performance is the primary objective.

So, if we place your performance level on the same 0- to 100-percent scale, we can rate how you really perform. If you manage to use every last little bit—100 percent—of your skill level on a consistent basis throughout a race, you can say that you performed at 100 percent, even though you may not have won or driven as well as Michael Schumacher would have in your car on that day. But you did perform at *your* 100 percent. That's the real goal. You can't, or shouldn't, ever be unhappy with performing at 100 percent. You may, however, make the decision to increase your scale. This is not done by wishful thinking, or more testosterone, or by trying harder! It is done only by implementing effective, efficient learning strategies. This is exactly what Aryton Senna did, and what Michael Schumacher does!

Obviously, though, if you didn't win (or even if you did), you will want to strive to improve both the competitiveness of your car and your own skill level. Although we won't go anywhere near a discussion of improving your car in this book, we will look at strategies that can improve your skill level. However, we won't take the traditional approach of covering braking and shifting techniques, cornering lines and such. Instead, we will develop strategies to implement and program these techniques.

We can tell a specific driver that he must have more patience, be less aggressive, brake later, be more consistent, produce better qualifying times, and so on. This diagnosis may be absolutely accurate, but it won't accomplish anything if we don't understand the programming process and help the driver know how to achieve these things.

## INNER SPEED SECRET #3

### Although your skill level may have physical limits, your mind's potential is limitless.

What we're talking about is an awareness, understanding, and implementation of ways to effectively and efficiently increase your skill level, and then to induce a preferred state of mind that enables you to access those skills at the highest possible level more frequently.

If you can acquire a better understanding of what causes your performance, great or crummy, you can develop better and more consistent performance strategies. Our goal for this book is not just to tell you what kind of attitude, mental preparation, and state of mind successful race drivers have, but how to get it.

# Chapter 2

# The Ultimate Management System

Today's top-level race cars have all sorts of data acquisition microsensors designed to gather information, and in some cases, to process that information and execute a change. Engines, whether in a Formula One car or your street car, are controlled by amazingly complex electrical engine management systems. These systems continuously monitor numerous parameters (throttle position, ambient temperature, exhaust temperature, air flow, rpm, etc.), and alter controls to maximize performance. The race driver's brain goes through a very similar process. The human brain is, in fact, the ultimate management system.

Throughout this book we will refer to, and compare the brain to a computer, as it does function in many ways like one. It is, however, very different than an IBM or Macintosh, because it is alive, And yet, the brain works like a computer. (Perhaps, as brains were here first, we should say that computers work like brains.) This does not mean that we are nothing more than a computer, but that we function in the same manner. We will, however, never lose sight of the fact that your brain is far more powerful, with far greater abilities, than any computer. For example, just one neuron (nerve cell) in your brain has the capability of one modern computer, while your brain contains approximately $10^{11}$ neurons, or about as many stars as there are in the Milky Way!

*Whether behind the wheel of a race car or not, your brain acts much like a very sophisticated computer.*

The total amount of information going into the brain while driving a race car is staggering to think about. If you could increase the amount of information by just 1 percent, would that increase your performance level? You bet it would!

While driving a race car (or doing anything, for that matter), information goes into your brain—your "biocomputer"—and like any other computer, that information is processed based upon your "software." A million-dollar, state-of-the-art supercomputer with no software will not do anything. Without software, it has no use! As well, software with glitches and bugs is often the cause of limited performance.

Your brain's software is an extremely complex organization of neuron patterns within the brain's cells. Years ago, researchers determined the "minimum number of patterns your brain can make is the number '1' followed by 10.5 million kilometers of typewritten zeros!" In other words, your brain's capacity is practically limitless. It is generally accepted today that the average person uses far less than 10 percent of the brain's capabilities.

This neuron patterning, or programming, is the basis on which you perceive the world around you. You cannot perceive anything based upon someone else's software. You cannot interpret based upon someone else's software. You cannot react based upon someone else's software. You cannot make decisions based upon someone else's software. One of your performance limitations is the quality of your mental software. Therefore, you need to develop your software to the level of performance that you desire.

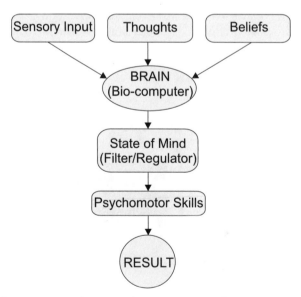

*As the flow chart suggests, information from your senses, thoughts, and belief system are input to your brain, where it is processed. The information is then filtered by your state of mind and sent to your body to be acted out (your psychomotor skills).*

As is true with any computer, the quality of information going into your brain is critically important. You may have heard the *GIGO* computer slogan, meaning "garbage in–garbage out." If a computer operator inputs poor-quality information, the result or output will be poor, whatever the quality of the computer's software or hardware may be. The same thing applies to your brain.

The basic process is simple: Information from your senses, thoughts, or beliefs goes into your brain, where it is processed, as with any computer, based entirely upon its software. And then, based upon the decision reached by your biocomputer (brain), your body (muscle by muscle, joint by joint, etc.) is given specific instructions (when to brake, how much to squeeze the brakes, how much speed to carry through a turn, when and how much to accelerate, and so on). Essentially, these are your psychomotor skills. As you will see, though, your state of mind—your emotions—can have a sort of regulatory or filtering effect on these psychomotor skills.

In reality, the process of controlling a race car obviously involves more than just your brain. It is a body-brain-body continuous loop that we are really talking about. Information from your body (senses) is sent to your brain, where it is processed, and then orders (bioelectrical signals) are sent to various parts of your body to be carried out. From there, more information and the reactions of those orders are sent back to the brain, new decisions are processed and sent back to the body again, and the loop continues.

As you increase your understanding of this process, you can begin to develop some strategies to improve your performance. First, you must understand the importance of developing the highest quality of information input.

## Processing Information

One of the primary differences between a great race driver and an also-ran is his ability to receive and process dynamic information. There are some other important differences, such as the ability to make good decisions and having a great skill level, which we will discuss later, but processing information is critical.

Think about everything involved in the act of driving a race car—or skiing, playing tennis, or a musical instrument, for that matter. Just imagine the millions of bytes of information that are being gathered by every part of the body, sent to the brain and processed, the electrical impulses that are then sent to the appropriate muscles to execute a specific movement, and then new information gathered, and so on. And all this is done in a few nanoseconds.

The more you practice receiving dynamic information, the more sensitive you become to gathering information. However, you do not gather and process information at a conscious level; it is done only at the subconscious level, which is, in effect, a part of your software.

## INNER SPEED SECRET #4

### Quality output depends on quality input.

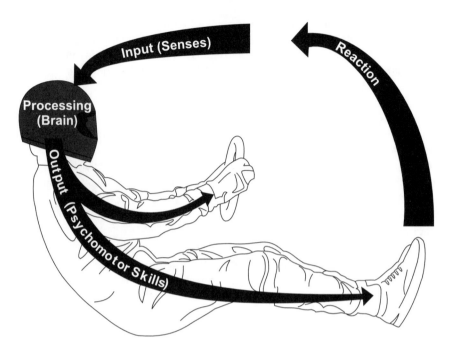

*The processing and acting upon of information is a continuous loop. Your brain re-ceives information (time to turn into a corner), it processes that information and sends a signal to your body (turn the steering wheel), makes note of the reaction (need to turn more), and the loop begins all over again.*

As an example, if we gave you a sheet of Braille, and an explanation of the patterns of raised dots, do you think you would be able to read the Braille right away? Probably not, because your fingers would not be able to recognize the patterns accurately. However, if you practiced it long enough, you could develop the sensitivity in your fingers to actually feel the tiny dot patterns and interpret their meaning. Developing that same high level of sensitivity in a race car is critical to performance.

So, one of the keys to being a quick race driver is to be able to gather dynamic information. And that takes practice. Practice becomes programming, and programming is your software from which your decisions and actions result.

A few years ago Ronn was working with an Olympic-level skier. She was a specialist in the giant slalom, but had developed a pattern of falling when she started going after more speed. Her skill and technique were not the problem. She had exceptional skill. He decided that to go faster, she needed more senso-ry input. One of the ways to do that was to get more auditory input into the brain.

So Ronn had her skiing many runs at lesser speed, with the primary objective of "listening to the sound of the snow." Just listening! She was, in fact, practicing getting more sensory input, which then allowed her to develop a program to get that additional auditory input at a subconscious level. The level of her skiing, and especially control, increased immediately. The falling pattern was broken, as she increased the ability to get more information into the brain.

Let's bring this back to racing and what you can do to improve. If you are able to do a testing program, it needs to be as effective and efficient as possible. Testing at any level of racing is expensive, especially if *you* are paying the bills! Testing should be more than just learning how the car will react to specific changes. It needs to be done with a total performance strategy, which includes practicing receiving information. Just look at it as developing a more sophisticated software program for the driver. This process will also increase your effectiveness as a test driver. A good test driver is one who has a high level of awareness (sensitivity), is able to create memory, and then relate that information.

Most race drivers are reluctant to suggest to their team that they would like to spend part of a test session working on developing themselves—particularly the mental aspects of driving—rather than developing the race car. Suggesting that you are working on a new line through a couple of the turns sounds more acceptable to the typical race team member than developing your sensory inputs. Most teams, however, believe a driver's ability is a given—"either you've got it or you don't." If only more team owners, managers, engineers, and mechanics understood how valuable and how much more efficient it is to work on developing the driver—and just how much a driver can improve, given the opportunity. This is especially true today with all the data acquisition systems, if the driver and the engineer understand what is happening. The driver has an even greater opportunity to create the memory of exactly what is happening at each segment on the track, and then relate that with the data acquisition information.

## How the Brain Receives Information

You drive a race car fast when you drive subconsciously—using a program (software). You cannot drive consciously—a race car is much too fast to operate on the conscious level. You must operate by a program. It is important to realize that we also need to gather information at the subconscious level. We cannot gather enough information at the conscious level. Our body's microsensors must be doing their job automatically.

The primary ways in which the brain receives information when driving is from three of the sensory inputs—seeing (visual), hearing (auditory), and feel (kinesthetic)—as well as through thoughts, emotions, and the belief system. The better the quality of input, and the more quantity of input, the better the output or performance.

Especially important to this process is the basic law relative to psychomotor skills that much of the programming in the brain comes about as the result of practice (repetitions) of the activity. Your programming is mostly a result of

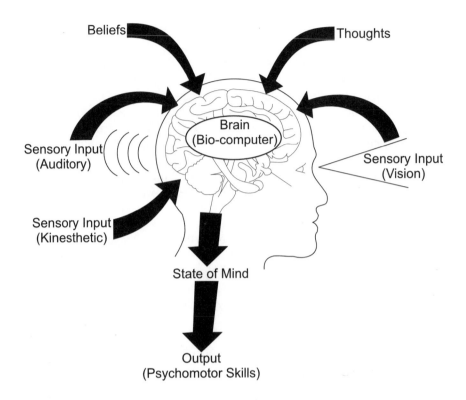

Beliefs

Thoughts

Brain
(Bio-computer)

Sensory Input
(Auditory)

Sensory Input
(Vision)

Sensory Input
(Kinesthetic)

State of Mind

Output
(Psychomotor Skills)

*Your brain receives information from a variety of sources.*

what you practice. If you practice (repeat) the right things, the right things will become programmed. If you practice the wrong things, the wrong things will become programmed. For this reason it is very important that you do not practice the wrong things. Whatever you are doing that is wrong must be changed as soon as possible. This is why strategies for practicing are not just important—they are critical!

Remember, practice doesn't make perfect. Only *perfect practice makes perfect.* We all should know this, but we tend to continue to practice some of the wrong things by repeating the same mistakes. Why? Probably because we don't have a very good learning, practice, or coaching strategy.

## INNER SPEED SECRET #5

### *Practice is programming.*

In order to improve as a race driver, the quality of sensory (visual, kinesthetic, and auditory) information is critically important. Fortunately, there are some exercises that can be used to increase the quality of the information gathered by your sensors.

## Strategies

As we mentioned in the Introduction, information and knowledge alone will not make you a better race driver. What you do with that information and knowledge—your strategies—is going to dictate your success. So, to relax and prepare your mind for the strategies presented throughout the remainder of this book, use the following exercises. These are also great exercises to be used regularly prior to getting into your race car.

### Neck Rolls

Roll your neck gently from side to side—first to one side, down (chin to chest), then to the other side and back down. Then do the same, only this time roll your head back instead of forward. Do not roll your head through 360 degrees; roll from the side, forward, to side—180 degrees, and then side, back, side—180 degrees. If you feel any tight spots, hold your head in that position for a few seconds until it begins to loosen.

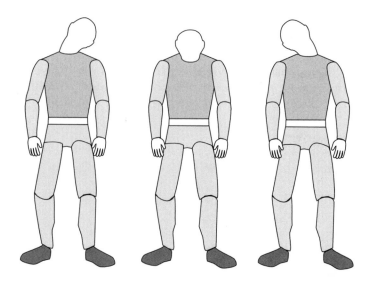

*The neck roll exercise.*

## Bracelets

Grip your arm below the elbow with the thumb and fore finger of your opposite hand, and turn. Continue turning as you spiral down to the wrist, massaging your forearms. This is a particularly good exercise for relaxing your hands and arms before and after driving.

*The bracelets exercise.*

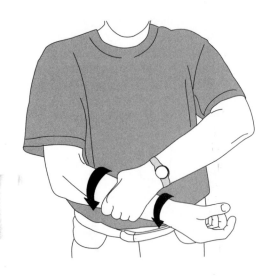

## Brain Buttons

With one hand, deeply massage the soft spots under your clavicle (to the left and right of your sternum, and just below your collarbone) for 30 seconds, while pressing your navel with the other hand. This not only helps you relax, but can also increase blood flow to the brain and improve brain-body bio-electrical communication.

*The brain buttons exercise.*

## Thinking Cap

Unfold and massage the curl in your ears using your thumbs and index fingers, beginning at the top and working down to your ear lobe. This improves your hearing sensitivity and concentration and helps you relax.

*The thinking caps exercise.*

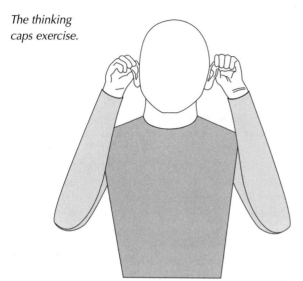

# Chapter 3

# Your Brain's Software

Practically everything we do is a result of a program, or the software in our mind. For example, if we asked you to go to the refrigerator and get a drink of milk, you wouldn't consciously have to think about moving your left leg in front of your right leg, then right leg in front of left leg, lift your hand to grab the door handle, and so on. Instead, you rely on the preprogrammed software in your mind that already knows the physical actions—the psychomotor skills—required to accomplish the task. Driving a race car works the same way.

Although we typically believe that we do most things by conscious thought, we really accomplish them—at least what we do well—subconsciously. When performing at your peak, your conscious mind sets the objectives and then leaves them for your subconscious mind to accomplish. When you try to do something consciously—thinking about it—you rarely perform at your peak.

You cannot consciously drive a race car fast. It is much too fast, and there are too many things happening too quickly for your brain to operate in the conscious mode. You must drive subconsciously, in an *automatic pilot* mode, everything happening as a result of the program.

# INNER SPEED SECRET #6

### Drive the race car on automatic pilot— subconsciously.

Consider what happens as a person learns to ride a bicycle. At first it is very difficult to keep your balance, but with practice it becomes easy. Once mastered, we never forget it. Then, even if it's 10 years since you pedaled a bike, you can ride almost as easily as when you last rode. Why? Every time you perform a task, such as riding a bike or driving a race car, certain neurons in your brain interact with one another and a neurochemical connection is formed. And, much as water flowing through dirt will develop a path and then continue to follow it, once that neurochemical interaction has occurred between brain neurons, the pattern of interaction will occur easily again. The skill of riding a bicycle has been imprinted on your brain; a program has been developed.

We need to look at learning as programming—to the deepest level. You have not really learned something until it is completely programmed to the subconscious level. Learning is not just being aware of something at the surface, or the conscious, level. For example, learning is not just being aware that

*I am able to get to a level where I am ahead of myself;
maybe a fifth of a second, who knows? When my car
goes into a corner, I am already at the apex.*

**—Ayrton Senna**

Turn 3 is a *late apex* turn, and that the absolute fastest line is exactly *this* path. Learning at the deepest level is the ability to take the car through the turn on *this* path, at the maximum speed at any point, without thinking about it at the conscious level. That is, it needs to happen *automatically*—at the subconscious level.

For the rest of this book, we need to ask you to look at learning in this manner. Learning is programming! Programming is learning! Substitute the word learning for programming, and vice versa.

How do we, as human beings, create these programs? We learn (program) little by reading about it. We learn (program) little by someone telling us to do something a specific way. Oh, we can memorize some information or figures, and then regurgitate them. But we learn to do something by doing it. We create our programming most effectively and efficiently through an experiential process.

Repetitions of this experience will create the programming into the subconscious. We are able to do something automatically—without thinking about it—as a result of creating the neuron patterning in the brain cells to execute a specific activity.

*Everything you do behind the wheel of a race car is a result of one of the countless number of programs in your mind. The key is selecting and fine-tuning the right program for the task.*

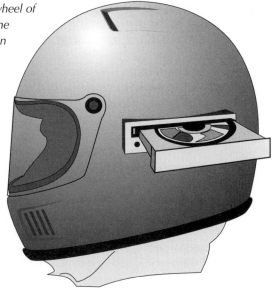

## Instant Replay and Preplay

In simple terms, the real purpose of your subconscious mind is to carry out and achieve the programs—the actions and objectives—at the direction of your conscious mind. If your conscious mind is focused on negative objectives, your subconscious will do everything it can to see you achieve them. If your conscious mind is focused on positive objectives, your subconscious will make them happen. So, obviously, what your conscious mind is doing is also extremely important!

The programs in your brain control more than your physical actions—your psychomotor skills. They also control your beliefs, thoughts, and state of mind. In fact, if a specific situation or condition triggers a state of mind program in which there is anxiety or fear, the performance level of the individual will decrease immediately. So programming exactly what you want to occur is critical! For various reasons, we frequently program many things we don't really want, especially during the learning process.

Programming a higher level of performance is often the result of deleting any programming you do not want (deprogramming), and reprogramming what you do want. Race drivers must have an understanding of what they are doing, what they need to change, what they need to do to change, how to change, and how that affects their resulting performance level. It isn't just a matter of wanting to do better.

Once you understand this, it gives a whole new meaning to the expresion *learning a track*. It isn't just knowing which turns are left or right, or increasing or decreasing radius, etc. And it is not just the basic general psychomotor skills of threshold braking at maximum level, or maintaining dynamic control at the very edge of adhesion while going through a high-speed turn, etc. It is the application of these skills, executed subconsciously at every segment of a track. This is really what learning a track is about. You must get to the subconscious level as quickly as possible. Then you can begin to work on observing what can be changed to be quicker, as you execute that new programming at the subconscious level.

Your brain is full of an uncountable number of programs, with an almost infinite number of complex combinations for everything from breathing to how to solve a complex math problem, from throwing a ball to talking. Obviously, we cannot look in detail at each separate program that it takes to drive a race car. (At least, not in the next thousand years!) But we can break them down into basic psychomotor skill programs and variations, or updated versions of the basic programs.

For example, once you've learned how to heel-and-toe downshift, and practiced it enough, you have developed a basic program for that psychomotor skill. If you drive another car on which the brake and gas pedal arrangement and the engine response are different, your basic program will have to be altered slightly. It doesn't mean having an entirely new program, just an updated version. (In computer software terms, call it version 1.1.) With every different car you drive, you have to develop a new version of the heel-and-toe program (versions 1.2, 1.3, 1.4).

*Nothing should be done in a hurry in racing, except the drive itself; for everything else you need calm.*

—**Alan Jones**

Until each psychomotor skill required to drive a race car becomes a fully developed program, you will not be able to drive at the very limit by yourself, let alone having sufficient brain resources left over to deal with the traffic and constantly changing conditions that occur when racing.

Hopefully, you can also see why the initial learning of a skill is so critical. If you try to drive too fast at the very beginning, you will not give your brain enough time to accurately develop the basic programs. And before you can develop the new versions of a program, you have to fully develop and de-bug the basic program.

As you will see, there is—or should be—an almost continuous programming/reprogramming process taking place whenever you drive. The better developed your basic program is, the more brain resources you will have in reserve to observe and suggest reprogramming alternatives or new versions. If all your brain-power reserves are being used to control your psychomotor skills, there will be none left to improve your functions. Now you see why it is so important to have effective programming techniques: Without a precise and accurate program, you will continue to do the same thing over and over again, never making any improvements.

The more variations of a basic program you have, the more adaptable and flexible you will be in unique situations, and the quicker you will learn new processes. It is astounding to observe how many race drivers, even drivers at the highest level, will try to force their car's setup (at that moment) to adapt to their personal driving style preference, rather than adapting their style (program) to what the car wants to do at that moment.

Rick Mears was one of the all-time best at adapting his style to suit the situation. He definitely had a knack for interpreting what was happening and what needed to be changed, and communicating that information to the team so they could make the necessary adjustments. As his record demonstrates, that usually resulted in as strong a finish as possible—often a victory in a car that didn't look to be capable of winning early in the race. Other drivers often try to make the car adapt to them, and in the process blister tires, scrub off speed, and perhaps lose control and crash.

As we said, once an action, movement, thought, or whatever is programmed into your brain, it is there forever. It may not always be easy to access the program, but it is there. Even a name or a face is a program. How many times have you not been able to remember a person's name—access the program—when you wanted to? Then, sometime later it just popped into your head. It was always there. You just had difficulty accessing it.

Usually it is when your mind is relaxed that you most easily access deep-rooted memories or programs. You often remember people's names when you are not trying to, right? What does that tell you about your mind when you're behind the wheel of your race car? It needs to be relaxed.

Some drivers just seem to have a certain intuition—an instinct or sixth sense—when it comes to racing. When you relax and trust your program—your subconscious—to drive, and stop thinking, you will too. Program your mind through mental imagery so that in racing situations, you respond instinctively. Remember the sayings, "Analysis is paralysis," and "Act, don't think."

*And that's what it's about. Trying to get the car to feel like part of your body. An extension. I get my mind into part of the machinery. And get it to be—like the tires are made of rubber, sure. But when things are right, you can feel the tires in your nerve ends. And when you take a car down into the corner as deep as it'll go and you know it's on the ragged edge, it's just like a shot in the arm. It's such a gratifying feeling that you've taken a piece of machinery and kind of glued yourself to it.*

**—Johnny Parsons**

You can develop the necessary programs either physically (through experience) or mentally (through thoughts, beliefs, and mental imagery). Both methods are effective in programming your brain, with each having advantages and disadvantages over the other.

### Physical Programming

Physical programming occurs through experience. It is the physical practicing of your psychomotor skills. For example, when learning to hit a tennis ball, your first hit usually isn't very accurate. Then, with each subsequent swing, your brain figures out through trial and error how quickly to move your arm, the arc it needs to follow to contact the ball, and the timing required. With more practice—physical programming—that movement becomes what tennis players call a *grooved swing*, which is really a basic program for hitting a tennis ball. However, as anyone who has played tennis knows, the ball rarely comes back to you at the exact same height, angle, or speed. So, you then practice (program) hitting the ball at varying heights, angles, and speed until you have a number of versions of the basic program, or variations of your standard "hit the tennis ball" program.

The same process applies to driving a race car. First, you learn the basic techniques (use of the controls, shifting techniques, placing the car along a desired path or line through a corner, etc.) until they become programmed. Then, while driving the race car by program, your conscious mind is watching precisely what the car and you are doing; and if the brain is not overloaded, it will notice slight variations that may enable you to go quicker. It then alters the program until you make an improvement, and makes that an updated version of the program. This is why seat time is so very important.

One of the problems with relying entirely upon physical programming is that while altering your program, you may make a negative change, resulting in a slower lap time at best or a crash at worst. On the other hand, sometimes errors actually lead to a positive update of the program. If you enter a corner too fast (failing to perform the *corner entry speed* program correctly), for example, and make it through the corner despite the extra speed, your brain has just learned that it can be done, so the process of reprogramming begins to update the necessary programs. The result is a new version of the program that increases your cornering speed.

Using physical programming can be dangerous, though. If you make a big change, such as turning into a corner 10 feet later, you may not survive long enough for it to become an updated program! On the other hand, if the changes you make are not big enough (turning in 1 foot later), your brain may just interpret that as your failure to perform the program properly, or that you are inconsistent.

In other words, to get the mind to accept something new, you may have to overcompensate. If you want to turn in 3 feet later for a corner, you may have to make a few laps turning in 5 feet later. Or, if you want to carry 2 miles per hour more speed into a corner, you may have to try carrying 3 miles per hour more for a few laps (even if that makes the car slide too much, resulting in actually going slower). Why? To move beyond an existing program in your mind, changing just slightly can fool the brain into thinking that it was simply a poor execution of an existing program. The result is not what is really required—a new program for turning in later, for example—but a program that says you are not performing the existing program well.

At a CART race in Australia several years ago, one driver was visibly slower in a very high-speed dogleg section. We are sure that the variance of his speed and other drivers' speed through this section was recorded on radar guns and with data acquisition. In one of the next practice sessions, you could literally see that he attempted to add far too much speed at one time. And we're also sure it was done with contracted muscles (from the tension of trying to make that big a jump in speed), which limits the quality of kinesthetic input and decreases the ability to be smooth, at the moment he needed to be absolutely smooth with all inputs. Net result: a very bad crash, which left him with injuries that could have been much worse.

Of course, physical programming costs a lot of money as well, as the only way to do it is by driving the race car. It also takes a lot of time.

## Mental Programming

There is a way of speeding up the programming/reprogramming process, and that is through the use of mental programming. It also improves the quality of the programs developed through physical programming. Practically everyone does this to some extent during various functions. Truly great athletes do it a lot.

One of the first benefits of mental programming is the cost—nothing! There is also no danger of making a mistake.

Essentially, mental programming comes about through the deliberate control and use of your thoughts, of taking charge over your beliefs, mental imagery, and the effectiveness of creating a virtual reality environment. We'll get into visualization, or mental imagery, in detail in chapter 5.

## External Programming

There is another type of programming, one that is mostly negative or counterproductive. External programming results from actions, words, and emotions from outside sources, namely other people around you.

Your subconscious mind is wide open to new programming, whether it comes from you or an outside source. This is why it is so important for the people around you—at the race track and away from the track—to understand the effect they can and will have on you. These people can include family, sponsors and their guests, crew members, team owners, managers, instructors/coaches, etc. It really is a shame that more race team owners and crew members don't recognize how just a simple word or two can have a drastic impact on the performance of the driver—if that driver does not have a strategy for dealing with it.

Of course, you can't just say you won't be affected by other people. You require an actual program to deal with external disruptions, distractions, negative emotions, energy, and dialogue. If someone says or does something that has a negative effect, you must have a peak performance program that automatically kicks in to block out the negatives.

You may think that you will be mentally tough enough to block it out by simply saying to yourself, "Don't let it get to you." Unfortunately, when you are even the slightest bit tired, or your confidence level has been tested by some recent results, you won't be able to without a preconceived program.

This is one of the primary reasons some teams of seemingly unbeatable talent don't live up to expectations. Often, one person will have a negative effect on another member of the team. And yes, you as the driver can have that same effect on other members of the team; and if they do not have a program to deal with it, their performance will suffer.

## Strategies

Using physical and mental programming, develop programs for various situations. By that, we mean use the time on the track followed by vivid mental imaging sessions to create set programs for the start of races, driving in a patient mode, assertive mode, qualifying mode, etc. Imagine what you would feel like, what you would see, how you would sound, how you would act in each of these modes.

## INNER SPEED SECRET #7

### Program your mind.

Then, *anchor* each of your programs. Use a *trigger* word or movement to signal the beginning of a program. That way, when you're in the car, all you need to do is recall the *trigger* to activate the program.

How do you do this? You will have to wait until chapter 5 for us to get to the details of how, for there is more background information to look at first—a few more balls to keep up in the air.

Through the years, we've had drivers comment that they don't like to think about their driving too much—they don't want to know as much as we are presenting in our seminars and in this book. Good! That means that they have complete faith or trust in their subconscious programs to kick in to enable them to perform well. However, as you know, the program must be a good program.

If you are one of these drivers who feel that all this talk about what is going on in your brain, or about the techniques of driving for that matter, will harm your performance, let us assure you that you are probably the one who can most benefit from some prior programming. Why? Because you already know how to let go and trust yourself to access and perform the program. Our point here is, with a little time and preparation, you can improve your programs—you can improve your performance.

# Chapter 4

# Brain Wave States

Just like a radio transmitter that generates radio transmission waves, your brain produces electrical frequencies. Doctors and researchers use an electroencephalograph (EEG) to measure these brain waves in terms of frequency (cycles per second or Hz) and amplitude (voltage). As you would expect, these oscillating electrical voltages are very low, just a few millionths of a volt.

Brain wave frequencies, or states, are divided into four levels:

**Beta** waves range between 13 to 40 Hz, or cycles per second, but are low amplitude. This is the range, or brain wave state, that we generally operate in most of our daily activities—the conscious state. It's associated with peak concentration, alertness, visual acuity, focus, and cognition.

**Alpha** waves range from 7 to 13 Hz, and are a little higher amplitude than beta. This is a state of deep relaxation, where we most effectively activate creativity. It is just below your conscious awareness, and is the bridge or link between your conscious and subconscious states.

**Theta** waves range between 4 to 7 Hz. You most often experience theta at that point where you are just drifting off to sleep, just waking up, and during light sleep. Your brain would also produce theta waves during meditation. This is your subconscious state. You are very receptive to information beyond your normal conscious awareness. In fact, some researchers believe the brain is in a *superlearning* state while producing theta waves.

**Delta** waves range from 0 to 4 Hz and are the highest amplitude. Delta waves characterize the deepest levels of sleep and your unconscious state.

An analogy for the four brain wave states is a four-speed gearbox. Delta, while you're sleeping, is like first gear. As you just begin to awaken, you shift into theta, or second gear. As you become more awake, you shift to third gear, alpha. And, as your day gets fully under way and you begin to concentrate, focus, and become fully alert, you shift into beta, or fourth gear.

Each of the four brain wave states is linked to a different level of consciousness, each being essential and good for a specific function. If, however, you cannot turn on a certain level of brain wave activity, you will suffer in some way. For example, if you cannot activate theta and delta brain waves, you will suffer from insomnia. People who can turn on and dial in their brain to the ideal state for the desired function are often considered to be gifted or talented.

Just as not using all four gears for acceleration would hurt a car's performance, not using all four levels of brain wave activity will hurt your performance. Unfortunately, many people do just that: They skip *gears*, operating only in delta and beta states. For example, an alarm clock wakes them from a deep sleep (delta). They are startled into being fully alert, and the stress of rushing to get ready for the day (along with the caffeine rush from a cup of coffee) bolts them directly into a beta state. Then, they spend the entire day rushing around, working, concentrating, and being stressed (beta), until they practically collapse back into a deep sleep in bed at night (delta).

These people usually wonder why they never seem to have the creative or intuitive brainstorms that other people do. The reason is their brain is never allowed to get into a state (alpha and theta) that will produce these thoughts, ideas, and inspirations.

If this person would just set the alarm 15 minutes earlier, and allow themselves to gradually wake up; give themselves time during the day to close their eyes and relax (reaching the alpha state); and then wind down at the end of the day and gradually fall asleep (experiencing theta), they would be far more effective in everything they did in a day.

Of course, for most people, the ability to switch or turn on the desired brain state is something they naturally learned as a child. Unfortunately, the hustle and bustle, the stress, and lack of time in many people's lives force them into almost forgetting how to produce alpha or theta waves. Not only does this reduce a person's performance level in practically all aspects of life, but it appears to harm the immune system as well, leading to health problems. For sure, stress and anxiety reduce levels of alpha and theta brain waves.

What does this have to do with driving race cars? First, researchers have shown that increased levels of alpha brain waves result in improved levels of creativity. Does race driving require creativity? You bet it does. Creative inspirations are preceded by a burst of alpha waves. Whenever you have a great idea, solve a problem, or figure out a way to get through Turn 3 faster, a burst of alpha waves occurred.

Second, sports scientists have also found that athletes produce more alpha waves just prior to peak performance. In fact, one of the differences between novice- and elite-level athletes is in their brain waves. A study of a particular group of athletes showed that as their performance improved, their level of alpha waves just prior to their best performance increased. This only makes sense, as we're sure you have at some time witnessed the relaxed, calm, and self-confident appearance of an athlete before a great performance.

What all this is telling you is that you need to practice putting your brain in an alpha and theta state. How? By spending time relaxing, visualizing (more about this in the next chapter), and allowing yourself to enter an almost meditative state.

## Strategies

As we said, one of the keys to a high-performance mind is the ability to control your brainwave states to your advantage—to be able to dial up more or less of the desired brainwave levels when required. Now understand that you are never just producing one level of brainwaves. Even in a fully alert, conscious state, some delta waves are being produced, and while in a deep sleep, your brain is producing beta waves. Being able to put yourself in a relaxed meditative state, increasing your levels of alpha and theta brainwaves, will improve your ability to mentally rehearse techniques and track layouts, and invoke appropriate beliefs and states of mind. Alpha brainwaves provide the strongest, clearest, and most effective visualizations.

### Alpha/Theta Brainwave State

So, how do you get yourself into a *receptive mind* meditative state? Try the following:

Start by sitting comfortably in a chair. Close your eyes. Take three or four deep breaths. Let your body relax. Starting at your toes and moving up to your head, let each part of your body let go—relax. Start counting your breaths. Focus on your breathing as it slows down.

After doing this for a few minutes, many people are ready to begin mental programming—their mind is in a receptive state. Other people require more time to slow down their mind. If so, continue counting your breaths—focusing only on breathing. Some people may find themselves almost falling asleep. If that's you, three or four quick breaths will usually produce an increase in beta waves, waking you up. You should now have discovered how to place yourself in a mental state ready to receive mental programming and imaging, which we'll look at in the next chapter.

Only you will be able to determine when you have slowed your mind down—when you have gone from a predominantly beta-producing mind to an alpha/theta-producing mind. As you perform this exercise more and more, you will learn to recognize when your brain is producing more alpha waves. When you are, you will know it—your mind will feel calm and still; you may have uninvited images that make no sense flash into your mind; and the outside world will fall away. Theta is that state you experience just as you come out of a deep sleep, where vivid and sometimes seemingly meaningless images pop into your head. It is also the state your mind is in as you drift off into a daydream.

With a little practice of this technique at home, you will find it easier and less time consuming to achieve that state at any time, whether on an airplane, in your trailer prior to a qualifying session or race, or even sitting in the race car on the grid.

## INNER SPEED SECRET #8

### *Practice relaxation.*

I n fact, one side benefit of using this technique prior to a race, for example, is that it gives your brain something to do other than get nervous. The relaxed, calm mind of athletes prior to great performances is a perfect example of the benefit.

So now you know how to place your mind in the ideal learning state—the perfect time for mental programming, or mental imagery.

# Chapter 5

# Mental Imagery

Over the last couple of decades or so, much has been made about athletes using visualization to improve their performance. What's all the fuss about? Well, your mind does not know the difference between a real and imagined, or visualized, experience. This is especially true if you can learn to involve all of your senses in the imagined experience. Therefore, it is possible—in fact, necessary and very effective—to get *seat time* in your mind's eye. In other words, visualize yourself driving the race car, and therefore, programming your biocomputer.

### Mental Imagery is Mental Programming

Mental imagery is simply a very effective and efficient substitute for a real experience, what we call a *mental equivalent*. If you close your eyes and imagine or visualize a specific place, thing, situation, or anything else, that is the information that is going into your brain. That is the information being processed. And your brain literally accepts that your experience is real.

Visualization is placing a picture, or a visual representation, of something into the mind. It is, in fact, sensory input into the brain. And, again, the brain just accepts the input as real. Surprisingly, some people don't believe in visualization when, in fact, many visualize every day—they just don't know it. In this case, though, it's called worrying. Visualizing negatively is exactly what worrying is. Worrying about something is having a mental image of something that has been, is, or will be negative. And it impacts the brain bioelectrically, slowing its speed of processing, and so on. It dis-integrates the brain's connection to the reciprocal side of the body; we lose balance, and we become less centered.

Take a moment, close your eyes, relax, and visualize a lemon, cutting the lemon in half and seeing the juice dripping from the lemon as you open it up. And then, in your mind, take a lick of the face of the lemon. When most people do this, they find that their mouth begins to salivate, because the brain believes that citric acid is on its way into the mouth, and signals are sent to the mouth to bring forth some saliva to counteract the citric acid.

Creating a mental image of doing something exactly the way you want to is a very effective learning strategy. In fact, it is sometimes better than actually doing it, because in your mind you can do it perfectly, and many times in a short period of time. Again, your subconscious mind does not know that you are not actually doing it. It is processing the situation, and establishing programming, as if you were actually doing it.

Race drivers who spend most of their days thinking about driving, such as the ones who work as instructors for performance and racing schools, are actually programming driving skills constantly. In this case, their thinking is a sort of mental imagery. Every time they think about, describe to a student, or observe a technique being performed correctly, more programming occurs.

There was a study done years ago using basketball players. Three groups of players were asked to shoot free throws to measure their success rate. One group was then asked to practice shooting free throws for 20 minutes per day. The second group did no practice whatsoever. The third group visualized successfully shooting free throws for 20 minutes per day. The result? The group that didn't practice, did not improve. The group that physically practiced improved 24 percent. The group that just visualized showed a 23 percent improvement.

The more senses you include in your visualization, the more effective it will be. Think of it as *actualization*, and use movement, hearing, feel—the more senses, thoughts, and emotions, the better you will be at mentally programming what you want. If you only *see* yourself involved in the activity, it will not be anywhere as effective as if you felt and heard the movement and the emotions that go along with it. In the example with the lemon, if you not only *see* the lemon, but you mentally *feel* the skin of the lemon, you mentally *smell* the juice of the lemon, you mentally *taste* the citric acid, you are creating a very effective virtual reality.

You can look at actualization as putting into the mind all types of sensory input—visual, tactile, auditory, and sometimes taste and smell—at the same time. With all of the senses involved, you are creating in your mind the closest possible thing to reality.

# INNER SPEED SECRET #9

## Program your mind with actualization.

M any people confuse daydreaming with visualization. However, there is a difference between daydreaming and mental imagery. Daydreaming has no objective—it is only wishful thinking. Mental imagery should always have a specific objective or goal.

Some people think that they are using visualization when they are just *thinking* about driving a track, or *thinking* about becoming more aggressive. That is not the same as being able to actually place yourself, your brain and your body, in a state so that you actually mentally experience the situation.

Since one of the keys to racing in the rain is simply learning to enjoy it, Ross particularly likes to mentally prepare or visualize rain driving while standing in the shower. Visualizing it while taking a pleasant shower puts him in a positive state of mind–the water falling down seems to trigger the same pleasant, enjoyable state of mind he feels when racing in the rain.

The effectiveness of mental imagery is limited only by your abilities to learn to *actualize*, or create a virtual reality, and by your imagination. You learn it the same way you learn anything else—practice, practice, practice! The cost per lap is sure right. It does take practice, though. And the more you practice, the more effective it will be.

The wonderful thing is that you can do a lot of programming without making mistakes. If you find that you are making mistakes, or running off the track, or locking up the brakes while doing mental imagery, stop! Programming errors will result in being good at making real errors on the race track.

## Race Modes

Mental programming is the *preplay* in your mind of various potential situations and conditions so that at any given moment you will have a program to recall and use, at the automatic level. A good example of this is what we call R-1, R-2, and R-3 modes.

In the Monaco Grand Prix in 1988, Ayrton Senna was driving at a "magical" level, even for him. He had out-qualified the entire field, including his teammate, Alain Prost, by over a second. By the 67th lap of the race, he had built up a 58-second advantage over Prost, who was running second. You could literally see that he was on the very edge of control while exiting each corner, and yet was never out of control. Every placement of the car looked to be consistent, and it was obvious to everyone that he was in the zone. He was coming within inches of the barricades on every exit, accelerating with absolute smoothness with never a bobble.

Then the team let him know of his substantial lead, and told him to slow down. But he chose to maintain his pace. A few laps later, the team instructed him to slow down, which he did, whereupon he immediately crashed into a barrier on the exit of the turn before the tunnel.

What happened? He was totally in the zone, in the flow, and in a deep level of concentration, and then suddenly crashed. We believe that this is what happened: Upon orders from the team to slow down, he went from driving at the total subconscious level to attempting to drive (slower) at the conscious level. He did not have a program to drive at another (slower) level, and his performance immediately disintegrated by attempting to drive at the voluntary level.

This is why we believe that drivers need to develop an R-1, R-2, and R-3 program for each segment of every track they drive. This becomes a very impor-tant strategy that the driver can implement at the right moment. What is R-1, R-2, and R-3?

### R-1

Driving at 10/10ths, pushing to the very limit, or as close to that as possible (subject to the car's systems). There are times when a driver needs to be at 10/10ths–qualifying, in pursuit of passing another car as quickly as possible, to defend a position by stretching a lead, and so on.

Unless you are totally in the zone it is very difficult to drive at 10/10ths for a long period of time. If you are leading with another car right behind you, and if passing is not likely outside of the racing the line, you may choose to run at R-2 in order to decrease the likelihood of a mistake. But watch for the other car in the braking zones, because that may be the only opportunity for him to pass. So, you may choose to be at R-1 at the entry and go through the turn at R-2 in order to save tires and fuel, and at the same time protect your position.

## R-2

Driving just slightly off of the R-1 pace. Brake points are just a few nanoseconds earlier, shifting is just a few rpm sooner, and the rotation of the car is just a little smoother since it is not on the ragged edge. You may choose to use R-2 in several situations. In practice or testing, you may want to establish a consistent *baseline* from which to see what any changes made to the car do. (If you are at the very edge of control, little mistakes here and there may not give you the clarity you need to read what the car is doing.) During the race, you may want to save tires, fuel, and your own physical and mental energy. You can never tell when getting just one or two more laps out of your fuel will give you an advantage if a caution period occurs. Running at R-2 can make a real difference in saving your tires.

## R-3

Driving just slightly off R-2 pace. Brake points are just a little sooner, shifting may be a few hundred rpm sooner, and your objective through turns is to be as smooth as possible to save tires and fuel, and especially to give a larger margin to lessen the chance of making an error. You may choose to use R-3 if your car is just not handling at that moment in the race, when your position can be protected, and there is not enough time to make up the distance to gain the position in front of you within acceptable risk, etc.

The primary objective here is to create a program for R-1, R-2, and R-3 so that you can execute based upon the strategy that the moment dictates. Each braking area, each turn-in, and each acceleration out of a turn needs to be rehearsed in the mind so that you know exactly what to do and how to do it, automatically, so that you don't have to think about it. All you have to do is make the decision as to the appropriate program.

## Strategies

As a strategy, sit down at home, or even better, actually in the race car (even up on jack stands in the garage), and do some very effective and cost-efficient programming through mental imagery. Create in your mind the total movement of the car through a segment of the track that you feel you can improve. See, feel, and hear yourself execute the mechanics of braking, steering input at the smoothest level, and smoothly squeezing on the throttle as the exit opens. Be aware of exactly the way you want to do it. When you go onto the track, your brain and body will be able to execute the segment at the subconscious level. Then you can refine the segment further.

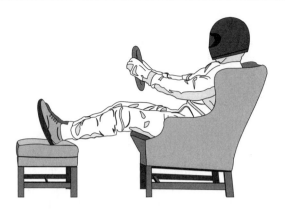

*For the ultimate effectiveness, it's important to get into a relaxed state prior to using mental imagery, and to make it as real as possible. Wear your helmet, hold a steering wheel, hear the engine, feel the car.*

Prior to beginning your mental imagery session, you want to allow your brain to get to the alpha/theta brainwave state you practiced in the last chapter. An alpha/theta state, as you now know, is simply a *superlearning*, super receptive state of mind, in which the brain will program at a much faster rate.

Now that your mind is ready, you can develop many ways to program what you desire. As an example, visualize that your whole body (as you sit in the car) has multiple little microsensors on your skin (on your legs, thighs, buttocks, etc.), and as you drive the car, you see and feel these microsensors sending huge amounts of information to your brain. While your mind is in slow motion, the sensors are sending the information in nanoseconds, and you are totally aware of feeling every piece of dynamic information as you drive around the track. You feel the centrifugal force as you go around the turns. You feel your hands and arms moving very smoothly, with total control of steering input and feedback. You feel the dynamics of the car, the weight transfer, the braking forces as you squeeze the brake pedal at the threshold level, and then ease off the brakes as the front of the car sets into the rotation for the turn, and then squeeze the throttle as the exit of the turn opens into the next straight.

Mental imagery is not just for programming technique, though. It can and should be used to program states of mind, beliefs, behavioral traits, thoughts, feelings, emotions—your entire mental mind-set. It can also help make goals and objectives more real and achievable by developing very clear mental images of them.

## INNER SPEED SECRET #10

### Use mental imagery to program your entire mental mind-set.

Some people feel they are incapable of visualizing, or that they are not very good at it. Some people are only able to visualize for a few seconds and then their image disappears. As we said, mental imagery takes practice; if you are capable of worrying about something, then you are able to visualize! When you practice mental imagery, if you can only visualize for a short period of time before thinking about something else, that's okay—you did it. Just focus again on your breathing, on getting back to an alpha/theta state, and do it again. With each time you will get better and better, and soon your mental imagery will be very vivid, detailed, and effective.

Every person visualizes differently. There is no right and wrong when it comes to mental imagery. Some people see themselves driving the car from their eyes' point of view (much as a helmet-mounted camera would see it). This is called Internal Imagery. Others see themselves from the outside (the way a TV camera or spectator would see them)—External Imagery. Is one way better than the other? Not necessarily. Some researchers feel that Internal Imagery may be more effective than External, but for the ultimate results in mental programming, it is best to do it both ways and even combine the views.

You can also visualize in slow, real, and fast motion. Slowing your imagery down allows you to work out the technical details. Fast-speed imagery gives you the chance to safely overcompensate the sense of speed and traction, so that when you are actually in the car, the speed will feel slow and comfortable. Imaging in real time puts it all together, and can be a good indication of the accuracy of your mental imagery. Using a stop watch to time a mental lap, you should be able to get within a second or two of your actual, real lap times.

Then—and this is a critical component—make a trigger or anchor part of your mental imagery, something that will trigger the desired program. For example, as you are actualizing driving a perfect lap, give the steering wheel two quick squeezes. Now, when you are in the car and you squeeze the wheel twice, that should trigger a state of mind capable of executing a perfect lap. Or, to get yourself in the right state of mind, visualize yourself in that state while thinking of a word, name, or phrase—anything that will trigger the ideal response when in the car. A trigger that has a strong emotional tie to your program will be most effective, and will require the least number of repetitions to activate the program.

A few years ago, Ross coached a very talented young driver in his first season of racing, competing in a spec series. "In the first few races he finished third and fourth, which was very good considering his experience level. But I knew there was more there—I had seen flashes of brilliance, and knew if he put it all together he could easily win. During the warm-up laps for his fifth race, it began to sprinkle rain. I went up to talk to him as he sat on the grid, where he had qualified fourth. This driver's hero was Michael Schumacher, so I asked him to imagine how Schumacher would handle the race. I kept calling him 'Schuey,' wished him luck, and walked back to where his family was watching. I said to them, 'Watch this.' I knew that this was it, I could see it in his eyes. He was

'Schuey.' By the second lap he was in the lead, and he continued to pull away, until he had more than a half-lap lead at the end of the race—and these were equal, spec cars! Obviously, we continued to use 'Schuey' as his trigger. Boy, did it work!"

You can play out hundreds, if not thousands of scenarios to prepare for the start of a race or passing opportunities. The more options you explore mentally, the better prepared you will be in the car. It's critical, though, to keep a sort of open-ended image of racing scenarios, because you will never be able to predict and visualize every possible scenario. The key is to be mentally prepared for whatever happens. In fact, that should be part of your mental imagery—being ready for every and any possibility, and reacting appropriately.

Definitely program your R-1, R-2, and R-3 modes, and keep updating them as your personal skill and performance levels improve.

And remember, if mental imagery works in a positive way, it goes without saying that it will work in a negative sense as well. In other words, if you visualize negative thoughts or results, or making mistakes, you will be programming them. Obviously, this is to be avoided. As soon as a negative thought or image enters your mind, you need to either stop your mental imagery or trigger a positive image.

Now that you know the most effective way to use mental imagery, begin to develop programs, not just of driving technique or possible scenarios you might face on the track, but how you feel and act, your beliefs, and your state of mind.

## INNER SPEED SECRET #11

*If you can't do something in your mind—in your mental imagery—you will never be able to do it physically.*

# Chapter 6

# Brain Surgery

To further understand how your brain ultimately affects your performance behind the wheel of a race car, let's do a little brain "surgery," looking at the various parts of the brain and what they do. Obviously, there is not much point in doing a detailed medical study of the brain. But, just as having an understanding of how a race car works makes you a better race driver, so will a little knowledge of your ultimate management system.

The better your understanding of how your brain functions, the more likely it is that you will implement some of the strategies that we will present. Few people will accept doing something unless they know why and what to expect. So our objective is to teach you why, how, and what you can do about it.

As we mentioned earlier, your brain is made up of tens of millions of neural networks, all ready, willing, and able to do what they do best. Researchers talk about the brain being made up of three main sections: the back brain, the midbrain, and the cerebral cortex. In a nutshell (perhaps not the best use of words when discussing the brain), the back brain deals with the automatic functions ("fight or flight" response), the midbrain with emotions and feelings, and the cerebral cortex with thinking. That may be a bit of an oversimplification, but it will do for our purposes here.

The cerebral cortex is made up of two hemispheres, typically referred to as right brain and left brain. These two hemispheres are connected by a bundle of nerve fibers called the corpus callosum, which conduct and regulate the bioelectrical energy, and communication, between the hemispheres. Your performance as a race driver (and practically everything else) is greatly affected by the amount of bioelectrical energy flow between hemispheres.

Research has defined the functions of the right and left hemispheres of the brain. In the majority of people, the left side of the brain primarily deals with structure, detail, language, factual-based logic, the little pieces; the right side mostly deals with creativity, art, free-form, intuition, the big picture. It is estimated that approximately 15 to 20 percent of people are transposed, and process opposite to this.

Understand there is not an absolute division of duties. The right hemisphere does some left brain activities, and vice versa. It's just that the dominance of brain activity is split in this manner.

In addition, the left side of the brain controls the functions of the right side of the body; the right side of the brain controls the functions of the left side of the body. The brain and body connection is, or should be, a reciprocal activity. We refer to this as a bilateral or cross-lateral integration. If the brain/body connection

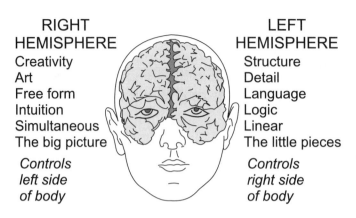

RIGHT
HEMISPHERE
Creativity
Art
Free form
Intuition
Simultaneous
The big picture

*Controls*
*left side*
*of body*

LEFT
HEMISPHERE
Structure
Detail
Language
Logic
Linear
The little pieces

*Controls*
*right side*
*of body*

*Your brain is made up of two halves, or hemispheres, each with its own duties.*

never became integrated—the flow of bioelectrical current between hemispheres being restricted—the person will probably go through life being uncoordinated and not know why.

Between the age of four to six months, most babies begin to crawl in a unilateral manner. That is, they crawl by moving the right arm and right leg together, followed by moving the left arm and left leg. At around six months, most babies begin to *cross crawl*—the right arm and left leg move together and the left arm and right leg move together. This cross-crawl patterning is absolutely necessary for the integration of right brain to left side, and left brain to right side. If the patterning does not happen, there will be some level of difficulty in coordination and balance. The problem becomes even more traumatic as it becomes a part of the young person's belief system: "I am not very coordinated! I am not good at sports!" A change in function and belief system at this point is a major challenge. But it can be done with appropriate strategies and implementation.

Recent research has defined what we have called *being in the flow,* or being able to perform at an extremely high level, as integrated, or operating with the whole brain. That is, the physiological reason for being in the flow is that the hemispheres of the brain—in fact all parts of the brain and body—are functioning together at the maximum level. This gives us the total information: the little pieces and the big picture; the structure and the free form; the details and the concepts; the automatic response and the higher reasoning.

Being in the flow is the result of being integrated, or whole brain functioning. What you really want, what will maximize your performance the most, is to operate in a whole brain mode; not allowing your back brain, your midbrain, your left hemisphere, or right hemisphere to dominate.

The opposite of this is also true. If there is something that affects the brain in such a way that one hemisphere or the other is functioning at a limited level, or that the communication between the two is restricted, the overall performance level is limited. This communication is directly affected by fear, anxiety, tension, anger, etc.—your state of mind—as well as many other factors.

# INNER SPEED SECRET #12

## Integrate to get in the flow.

Fear, anxiety, anger, doubt, etc. (for most people) causes dis-integration. The result is unilateral function–coordination, and balance is lost to some degree. So if you can do something to reintegrate (cross-lateral function), you can regain coordination and balance. You can regain integration of the right hemisphere and left hemisphere of your brain.

Your state of mind will limit, or filter, the access to your psychomotor skills. Although we have a tendency to place the state of mind into the realm of the psychological, the decrease in performance is the result of a physiological reason. Pressure, tension, anger, and anxiety are a form of fear, and these emotions will decrease the communication between the hemispheres of the brain. Again, the corpus callosum's function is to conduct bioelectrical energy between the hemispheres, so that the brain operates as a whole, or integrated. Your performance is the direct result of the increase or decrease of this bioelectrical energy.

As a race driver, you know how critical balancing the race car is to driving fast, or at least you should. Balancing your brain and body is just as important, if not more so. Your brain and body will be better balanced or integrated if you become more ambidextrous. What's so good about being ambidextrous? Well, look at what some great ambidextrous athletes including Michael Jordan, Larry Bird, Magic Johnson, Mickey Mantle, Willie Mays, Muhammad Ali, Joe Louis, and Sugar Ray Robinson achieved. Or artists Leonardo da Vinci and Michaelangelo.

Using your nondominant hand, for example, for simple activities helps activate the side of your brain that does not normally get used for those actions. The more both sides of your brain are exercised, the more integrated and balanced you will be and the better your performance will be.

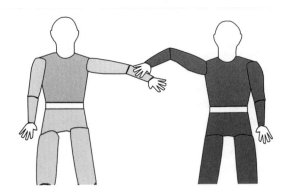

*Muscle checking is used as a form of biofeedback to determine the level of brain integration, or how switched on you are.*

So what, specifically, dis-integrates the brain or interferes with a person being integrated, or performing whole-brained? Many things can, such as your state of mind, belief system, thoughts, and even food and breathing (or lack of). We'll look at how to control these "dis-integrators" in their specific chapters, but first, how do you know if you are integrated or not?

## Muscle Checking

There is a fairly simple way of checking a person's level of brain integration. It is a technique called "muscle checking," and is used by kinesiologists, chiropractors, medical doctors, and researchers.

As it takes a fair bit of training to become competent at muscle checking, we will not go into great detail as to how you do it. However, it is very educational to understand what it demonstrates and why it works; and we will use it to illustrate a variety of integration and dis-integration factors.

To do a muscle check, the person to be tested stands with his feet shoulder-width apart and with a slight bend in his knees. He then extends his arm straight out to the side, parallel to the ground. A facilitator then presses down on the arm while the testee resists with only the deltoid muscle in the shoulder.

Now, this is not a muscle contest, but simply a way of testing the level of integration. The objective is for the facilitator to establish a benchmark or reference pressure with the application of firm, steady pressure on the outstretched arm. The testee is asked to relax and take a few deep breaths, and then the muscle check is performed. If the testee's arm drops, the muscle is switched off. If the arm stays strong, or locked, the person is switched on.

What does "switched off" and "switched on" mean? When the brain is integrated, the person is strong and switched on. When it is dis-integrated, the muscle will be weak or switched off.

The body never lies—it will give biofeedback of exactly what the body/mind is experiencing. This exercise gives an objective understanding of what actually happens as a result of your brain being integrated or dis-integrated. By the way, many doctors use this biofeedback test to check for everything from the exact point of an injury to allergies. It is very accurate.

Typically, in our Inner Speed Secrets seminar, we will perform a muscle check before and after each of the following scenarios:

- The facilitator asks the testee to "try—try real hard to keep the muscle strong."
- The facilitator asks the testee to "resist with power," or "do your best."
- The facilitator asks the testee to visualize a fearful, traumatic or unpleasant experience.
- The facilitator asks the testee to visualize a calm, relaxed, and pleasant experience.
- The facilitator says "boo!"
- The facilitator shows the testee a piece of paper with a large "X" on it.

What happens? With most people, when they "try," they become switched off; and when they "resist" or "do your best," they are switched on. Why? Because the brain simply does not understand "try." The brain understands doing something, or not doing something, but it doesn't understand the concept of "trying" to do something. Therefore, it is confusing, and the result is dis-integrating. "Trying" is also a negative thought. It suggests a chance of failing. "Resist" is positive. It is what you want to do—it is what you will do. "Trying" dis-integrates the brain, while "resisting" integrates it.

How many times have coaches said to their teams, "I want you to really try harder?" How many times have you said to someone else, or even to yourself, "I am going to try harder," or, "I am going to try to improve my qualifying time," or, "I am going to try to be more consistent." Not only does it fail to make any change, it actually applies more pressure, and then frustration, because you failed.

If at first you don't succeed, do not try, try again . . . and don't try harder! Get a strategy and make a change.

The difference between an imagined unpleasant experience and a pleasant one is much the same. The mental picture of an unpleasant situation reduces the bioelectrical flow between brain hemispheres, switching off or dis-integrating the brain.

This demonstration is very enlightening. Just the thought of a specific situation or the subconscious trigger of a prior traumatic experience can dis-integrate the brain to the point that your performance decreases substantially.

Over the years, we have worked with many drivers, both race drivers and street drivers, who have been involved in traumatic crashes. Many of them are driving today with these past traumatic experiences in their subconscious. Of course, every time something triggers the memory of the experience, they immediately become dis-integrated, and their performance suffers.

What about "boo"? Did it scare the testee? We doubt it, and that is why this is an interesting and surprising way to experience the effects of fear. For many people, somewhere way back in their subconscious or belief system, they relate the word "boo" with being startled, afraid, and tense. Again, that dis-integrates the brain. In fact, your belief system has a huge impact on your brain's level of integration.

If you ask someone being tested why "boo" has that effect, most respond by saying they were distracted. If the test is repeated but this time saying "banana," the muscle will test strong—most people like bananas. If they test weak, they don't like bananas. This is done just to prove that it is not a matter of distraction. It is totally dependent upon the representation of the word—what the word means to you. For most people, if you say snake, their brains will totally dis-integrate.

A few years ago, Ronn was conducting a seminar for race drivers in Ontario, Canada, and several drivers from Montreal attended. "I started with the 'boo' test with one of the French Canadian drivers, and it had no effect. At first I didn't understand, because I had never worked with a person with whom 'boo' didn't cause a weak muscle response. Then I realized, the word 'boo' has no meaning of fear to this driver, because of the language differences."

And the "X" on a piece of paper? The "X" is an ideal visual pattern for encouraging both hemispheres of the brain to act as a whole, or integrated. Conversely, two parallel lines (similar to an "11") can actually switch your brain off.

## Strategies

What all this muscle checking really does is give a few examples of what integrates and dis-integrates a person's brain. Although we will discuss some of these and other factors in the ensuing chapters, use the following strategies to help integrate your brain, balance your mind/body, and improve your ambidexterity.

## Centering

Place your tongue on the curve in the uppermost part of the roof of your mouth behind your front teeth (hard palette). This point is an accupressure point that the Chinese have used for centuries, and is used in tai chi. It is used to trigger integrated brain function.

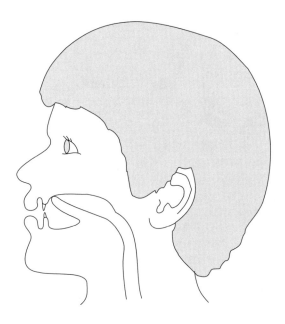

*To center yourself, place your tongue on the accupressure point on the roof of your mouth.*

**Cross Crawl**

While standing, raise your right leg, leading with the knee; as the knee reaches about waist height, touch the knee with your left hand or left elbow. Do the same thing raising the left knee and touching it with the right hand or right elbow. Begin a constant, smooth rhythm, so that you are challenging your balance. This is simply a cross-lateral walking in place that activates both brain hemispheres simultaneously, and increases the bioelectrical current flowing through the corpus callosum. Initially, this should be done slowly, which requires more fine motor involvement and balance. Then, have fun with it. Use it as a physical warm-up exercise. Lying on your back, do crossover sit-ups, touching the opposite elbow to the knee. You can even visualize it while sitting in your race car.

If a muscle check is performed after doing these cross-crawl exercises, your muscle will lock strongly. You are switched on—integrated.

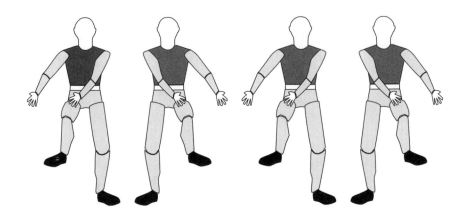

*The cross-crawl exercise.*

**Balance Buttons**

Place two fingers on the mastoid area (behind the ear, just above the indentation where your skull rests over your neck) while holding the navel with the other hand for about 30 seconds. Then do the same on the other side of your body. This exercise helps to become centered and balanced.

*The balance button exercise.*

## Hook-up

Extend your arms in front of your body with the palms out and thumbs facing down. Cross your arms together at the wrist, palm to palm, and interlink your fingers. Pull your hands down and toward the chest and fold upon your chest, with fingers under the chin. Then, cross your legs at the ankles. This has a similar integrative effect as the Cross Crawl exercise. It can be a great position for relaxation and while doing the mental imagery we presented in chapter 5.

*The hook-up exercise.*

## Nondominant Hand Lazy 8s

Draw a "lazy 8"—the figure 8 lying on its side—on a piece of paper with your nondominant hand. This exercise really helps you become more ambidextrous. Also do them with your dominant hand, practicing until both hands are close to equal.

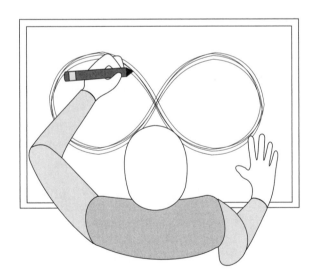

*The nondominant lazy 8s exercise.*

# Chapter 7

# Sensory Input

A s we said, the brain is basically a biocomputer, and the quality of information that comes out is based totally upon the quality of the information that went in, along with the software that processes that information.

## INNER SPEED SECRET #13

### The better your sensory input, the better your skills.

W hen it comes to driving a race car, people process most information in three primary ways—visual, kinesthetic, and auditory. At specific times, such as lunch, we use the other sensory inputs, taste and smell, but they have little to do with driving a race car, although the sense of smell is one of the most effective triggers for prior experiences.

Most people use either visual or kinesthetic as their primary processor. Auditory is the least effective for most people because they do not process a lot of information through their hearing. Have you heard the expression "It goes in one ear and out the other"?

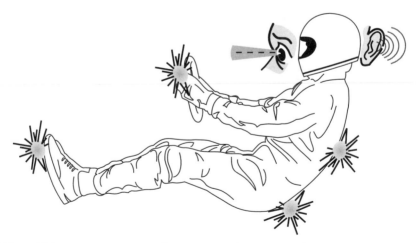

*When driving a race car, your primary sensory inputs come from your eyes, ears, and feel.*

Unfortunately, some teachers and school systems still rely almost totally upon the student's auditory sensory input, and wonder why the student does not learn (program) much. Research into super learning techniques has shown that if more than one processor or sense is used, the learning is much more effective and long lasting. Many of the problems associated with learning disabilities are simply the result of a student not using the appropriate sensory input, or not having developed the habit of using multiple sensory inputs.

During the past 10 years, we have had the opportunity to work with several hundred young people who have been defined as learning disabled. In fact, in almost all cases, a learning disability is considered as a *generic condition*, rather than a comprehensive diagnosis of the real cause of the difficulty in learning.

In more than half of these cases, the primary causes of their learning difficulties are found in visual processing problems (visual spatial awareness, visual tracking, visual integration, etc.) or in limited right side/left side brain integration, resulting in a lack of coordination, balance, multitasking, maintaining focus, etc. That is, the problem is often not a brain function limitation (hardware), as much as it is an input problem. Unfortunately, no one had ever diagnosed the cause of the problem; and in many cases, these people have spent years in special education programs, and now have a belief system that they are not very intelligent.

Our ability to learn is greatly enhanced if we can process information using as many sensory inputs as possible, and especially through experiential learning. The more senses that we can involve in a learning process, the more effective the learning (programming).

When working with performance strategies, a race driver should be intensely aware of learning strategies, and should focus on being able to see what the car is doing—to feel what the car is doing—and to hear what the car is doing. The most effective learning is through experiential learning. The more we experience through our senses, the more effective the learning.

## Visual Input

Driving any vehicle should involve all three sensory inputs, although visual input is obviously the most important. Since the primary sensory processor used in driving is visual, the development of quality visual input is very important. This is especially true when you consider how you must be able to identify and predict what all the other cars on the track with you are doing or what they are going to do.

There is a big difference between good eyesight and good vision. What we typically refer to as good eyesight is what your doctor tests with an eye chart. It is your ability to see something with clarity—your central vision acuity. Vision encompasses many things, but primarily it is your ability to observe things. It is mostly what your brain does with the information input from your eyes. In fact, research has shown that only 4 percent of what you perceive is the result of your eyes (sight); the other 96 percent is manufactured in your brain (vision).

We usually think of visual information in terms of visual acuity—what you can see (the ability to focus while reading, at a distance, or the ability to see at night). However, the quality of visual information is much more complex than just that. Good vision—visual awareness—is a prerequisite for being able to drive competitively. Most people wrongly feel they have the visual skills that they were born with and nothing can be done to improve them. Vision skills, however, can be improved through specific exercises.

Part of good vision techniques also comes from what we call *visual recognition*. As an example, while driving down a highway, most people can tell you the name on a restaurant sign well before they can clearly see the name. That's because they have seen the name many times before, and as soon as the eyes report the shape and color of the sign to the brain, it recognizes it. You could call it visual memory, and it is something you rely on heavily in racing when identifying other cars, reference points, and so on.

The physiological function of the eyes is obviously important, but in regard to driving, it is critical. If there is physiological deterioration that has resulted in extremely poor quality of visual information, the driver simply cannot see well enough to drive competitively.

For this reason, we recommend a periodic visual screening through a complete evaluation, preferably with a sports vision doctor; testing for vision acuity, visual field screening, depth perception, contrast evaluation, binocular fusion, and ocular motility assessment. For younger drivers, there is really no need to require a visual evaluation any more often than every couple of years. For drivers over the age of 40, the visual evaluation should be more frequent. One of the primary sources of visual problems occurs as a result of the aging process. As a person gets older, the eyes require more illumination in order to see at the same quality level, and they tend to track a moving object with vision acuity (by turning their head) rather than maintaining the quality of peripheral vision. And, if a driver has had a head injury, he should have a complete visual evaluation immediately.

Becoming aware of your strengths and weaknesses through periodic testing gives you the opportunity to do some proactive visual exercises to improve your driving and prolong your racing career.

As you can see (no pun intended), driving a race car doesn't just require good eyesight, it demands good vision.

## Kinesthetic Input

We typically refer to the kinesthetic sense as "feel" or "tactile." This is the overall sense of feeling exactly what the car is doing: the dynamics, weight in motion, vibrations, forces and strains, potential loss of control, and most important, traction sensing.

The quality of kinesthetic information while driving a race car is very important; it is absolutely critical in regard to your performance level. We typically refer to this as "seat of the pants" feel for what is happening, hence the need for more *seat time*. However, you can develop strategies to increase the amount and quality of kinesthetic information if you have a more complete understanding of the system and the process.

If you can increase the quality of kinesthetic information going into your brain, you can improve your driving performance. You know that the balance of the car is important to its traction and cornering grip. Improving your sense of balance, and not doing things that hurt your balance, is critically important, so you will be sensitive to the car's balance.

The only way that you can develop a high-quality level of kinesthetic processing is by doing—by experiencing, by practicing, by exercising the body's kinesthetic sensors. As an example, many drivers learned something about skid control and skid recovery by going out and putting a car into a skid on snow and ice in a parking lot, or on a dirt road. This is the only way to learn how to do it. The problem is that in the absence of a controlled and safe environment or a skills training program, this is a very dangerous way to try to learn the skill.

Very often, the difference between an average driver and the elite driver is a very small percentage. For this reason, a quality driving school or coaching session may be a very good investment for the race car driver. Most race drivers would benefit immensely from time spent on a skid pad. It amazes us how much time, money, and effort are spent on improving the race car, and how little on something as simple as a session on a skid pad for the driver.

Kinesthetic information travels to the brain through three individual but related systems: the vestibular system, the proprioceptive system, and visual processing. Since this book is not intended to be a textbook on the neurological function of the brain and body, we won't go into the science. However, it is important for you to have an awareness of the basic process, if you want to implement some strategies to increase your performance.

### The Vestibular System

The vestibular system, located behind the earlobe in the mastoid bone, controls your sense of movement and balance, and maintains both static and dynamic equilibrium. Static equilibrium refers to the orientation of the body—mainly the head—relative to gravity when you are standing still. Dynamic equilibrium, or balance, maintains body position in response to sudden movements such as acceleration, deceleration and rotation when you are in motion, as when walking or driving. This is especially important in an extreme dynamic environment such as driving a race car.

### The Proprioceptive System

Often referred to as our sixth sense. As far as driving a race car goes, along with your sense of balance, this is where much of the so-called seat of the pants feel comes from. G-forces, for example, are sensed through your proprioceptic receptors as forces pulling and pushing against your skin, muscles, tendons, and bones, and this information is communicated to the brain. The processing of this system must occur almost instantaneously.

### Visual Processing

Information from your eyes also contributes to your sense of balance and equilibrium. In fact, about 20 percent of the input from your eyes goes to an area of the brain that deals with balance. There it is checked and compared to information from your vestibular and proprioceptive systems.

### Auditory Input

The quality of auditory information while driving is important, but it is not as critical as is visual and kinesthetic information. In fact, a hearing-impaired person can get a racing license; a blind person, of course, cannot. The hearing-impaired person does, however, need to compensate for the lack of auditory information by increasing the effectiveness of the other senses.

One of the best ways to get a better understanding of the importance of this is to imagine playing tennis without auditory input. If you cannot hear the sound from the ball being hit, you simply don't have as much information—your ability to estimate exactly when and where the ball will be will suffer.

As the example of the downhill skier mentioned in chapter 2 suggested, spending practice time concentrating on improving auditory input can greatly enhance an athlete's performance level. Focused and concentrated strategies to control the impairment and improve the quality and quantity of all sensory inputs is the key.

Since your hearing is so important to driving a race car, it should be common sense, then, to protect yourself from hearing loss. Race cars are loud, and unless you have protection, they will damage your hearing. Hearing protection, in the form of ear plugs, is inexpensive and easy to use. With any amount of hearing loss, your performance as a race driver will suffer.

### Strategies
#### Sensory Input Sessions

To improve the quality of your sensory inputs, try the following:

During a test day or race weekend, take a session or portion of a session to only hear the car and track. Make note of every sound—the exhaust note, engine mechanical noises, tires gripping the track surface, chassis bottoming out against the track, etc.

Then, use a session to just feel the car and track, making note of the g-forces against your body, the amount of body roll and pitch the car experiences, the tires as they grip the track and then begin to slide, the amount of flex in the tire sidewalls, how harsh or soft the car feels going over bumps on the track, how quickly the steering response is, the vibrations and feedback through the steering wheel, the vibrations in the brake pedal, and so on.

And finally, spend a session focusing on what you can see, such as every little crack and undulation in the track surface, the direction your visual point of view changes as the car rotates and slides, where you can see other cars on other parts of the track, etc.

Doing these exercises will make you much more sensitive to what the car is doing, and improve the quality of input to your brain. Again, the better the quality of input, the better your output (skills) will be, not to mention your becoming a better test and development driver.

*Vision Exercises*

The primary strategy used to increase the quality of visual information is typically through the use of specific types of lenses for eyeglasses, which impacts visual acuity only. However, it would be a good investment of time and money to counsel with a good sports vision therapist in regard to your specific situation, and to develop visual exercises that will help you maintain quality vision for the long term. This should be done as a *proactive* (preventative) program rather than a *reactive* program. Vision therapy is very effective!

We tend to think that if we open our eyes, we all process the same visual information. This is simply not the case. Visual integration of information into the brain is very important at racing speed, and the processing of visual information is very complex. This is why vision therapy works so well.

**Focus Stretches**

Raise one hand in the thumbs-up position and hold the thumbnail in front of your nose and focus on the detail of the thumb. Then select an object at a medium distance (10 to 15 feet), and focus immediately on that object. Next,

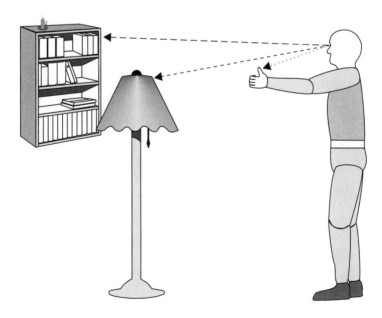

*The focus stretch exercise.*

select an object at a greater distance, and focus immediately on that object and then back to your thumb, etc. Repeat for two or three minutes. This will help retain flexibility and elasticity of the eyes' lens. You can imagine how important this is in the race car.

An option on this exercise involves taking a 10- to 12-foot length of string (preferably about the thickness of yarn), put four or five beads evenly spread onto the string, and tie at both ends. Tie one end to a door knob, hold the other end with your thumb and forefinger, and pull taut to just below your chin. Focus your eyes upon first one bead and then another, moving your focus to a new bead about every second or two. You should see two strings coming into the bead and two strings exiting the bead. If you see only one string going in or coming out in any position, one eye is severely dominating the other (the Lazy 8s exercise in chapter 18 will help correct this). This can lead to problems in closure speed and distance. As you proceed with the exercise, if your eyes are integrated, it will seem as though the eyes are almost operating like a zipper, going from one bead to another.

**Peripheral Stretches**

Place both hands together and in the thumbs-up position, with your arms fully extended. Then, slowly rotate your arms in the opposite directions on the horizontal plane toward your sides until you lose sight of your thumbs. Bring them back to center again. Do the same thing on the vertical plane, moving one hand up and the other down.

The peripheral stretches exercise.

## Auditory Exercises
### Layered Listening

Listen to all the sounds around you. At first you'll hear the most obvious sounds—car sounds, people talking, etc. Keep listening. Soon, you will notice the next layer of sounds—your breathing, noises off in the distance, etc.—the less obvious sounds. Keep listening still. Keep working at hearing the next layer of sound until you hear the sound of your own heartbeat.

## Kinesthetic Exercises

Although there are no physical corrective measures you can do for your kinesthetic sense, there are, just like with vision and hearing, exercises to improve theses senses. Besides spending quality time practicing on the track and a skid pad, see the Traction Sensing exercises in chapter 18.

In addition, balance is a very important part of the total kinesthetic input. Balance, or centeredness, comes from a total integration of the hemispheres of the brain to the reciprocal sides of the body, as we mentioned in the last chapter.

# Chapter 8

# *Thoughts*

Whatever you are thinking about will be processed by your biocomputer; and based upon your brain's programs and the thought, a physical movement (psychomotor skill) will be acted out. Our thoughts can come from a conscious decision to think about something, or they can be triggered based upon a prior experience, especially a traumatic one.

## *INNER SPEED SECRET #14*

### *What you think about is what you get.*

As we have addressed, the quality of the information going into your brain while driving is critical. Therefore, the quality of each information source, including your thoughts, must be considered, and strategies for improving the quality must be developed. Of course, there are many things that impair the quality of

*You need a strategy, or program, to not think about elephants while driving.*

your information input, such as prescription drugs, alcohol, fatigue, anxiety, and other emotional states, that should be avoided.

The most important concept for you to understand about thoughts is that you cannot *not* think about something. For example, while reading this paragraph, do not think about a bright pink elephant. Do not think about it! We said don't think about a pink elephant!

What happened? You thought about a bright pink elephant, right? As we said, you cannot *not* think about something. What you can do, though, is have a strategy to think about what you want. If, for example, you have a strategy of thinking about smooth driving whenever someone mentions pink elephants, then you will think about what you want to think about. It's all about having a strategy.

## INNER SPEED SECRET #15

### You cannot not think about something.

### Strategies

Practice focusing on what you want to think about, and not what you don't want to think about. The key is to have something—a preplanned thought or program—always on standby, ready to kick in whenever an unwanted thought enters your mind. For example, your preplanned or programmed thought may be of how much you enjoy the feeling of driving a race car at the limit. Then, whenever an unwanted thought—worry about budgets or money, what would happen if you crashed, something distracting a crew member said, and so on—enters your head, use it to trigger your preplanned thought. Develop this strategy using mental imagery.

# Chapter 9

# Belief System

Your personal belief system has one of the most critical effects upon your overall performance, especially in high-stress and pressure situations. If a driver believes that he is not a good driver, or that in a specific situation he will lose control, or that he is not good in a crisis situation or a hazardous driving condition, that is a part of his programming. And that programming can be changed only by changing his skill to the level at which he changes his perception and becomes confident in his ability, or by changing his belief system through reprogramming.

A person's belief system is different from his *ego* system. The ego system is often a reflection of a person's insecurities and behavioral issues, with the person frequently trying to convince someone (sometimes himself) that he really knows what he is doing, or that he really is confident or good at something. Usually, the person who talks consistently about what he has done does not have a strong belief system; he has lots of insecurities. The belief system is down underneath all of that—the real stuff!

Often, beliefs are limitations. Running the mile in under four minutes was for many years believed to be impossible. Then, once the four-minute mile was broken, runners everywhere were doing it. Did the physical abilities of all these runners improve all of a sudden? No, only their beliefs. It took one person to prove it could be done to change everyone's beliefs.

We work with a lot of race drivers and other athletes in developing strategies to impact belief systems that cause limitations in their performance. As an example, many race drivers believe that they are not good in the rain. For a road racer, obviously, this is not a good thing. If the race driver believes that he is not good in the rain, he contracts muscles, holds his breath, dis-integrates his brain, loses a substantial amount of his kinesthetic input (at the time he needs it most), and his performance level decreases. And as this happens, deeper programming of "not being very good in the rain" is created.

To illustrate the power of a person's belief system, consider the following. It is a well-known scientific fact that caffeine is a stimulant that disrupts sleep. In a study done years ago, subjects were given either coffee or milk just prior to going to bed. The next morning the people who drank coffee complained of not being able to get to sleep, while the people who had the milk claimed to have had a great night's sleep. Unknown to all the subjects of this study was that the caffeine had actually been removed from the coffee and added to the milk! Of course, the subjects believed the caffeine would keep them awake and the milk would help them to sleep. The belief system is so fantastic that it can overpower even the chemical reactions of a drug.

In our Inner Speed Secrets seminar, when Ronn begins a discussion regarding the belief system, he starts with a proposal to go out to the swimming pool at the hotel, and see if we can walk on water. In some cases, perhaps, he is perceived as a unique enough person that participants really wonder if they are going to attempt to walk on water.

Then he will ask how many people believe that someone just might be able to walk on water. Not surprisingly, no one buys into anyone being able to do that. Their belief system just can't accept that this is a possibility. So on a continuum line of beliefs, Ronn places "walk on water" way out to the right. Then he asks, where on that continuum line would building a huge fire in the parking lot that evening, placing the white-hot coals into a solid strip about 30 feet long, pulling off their shoes and walking on the coals be? How many people believe that could be done?

Invariably, although some people have no interest in doing it, many people believe that it can be done. When Ronn asks how they can believe that walking on 1,500 degree, white-hot coals barefooted can be done without burning their feet, the answer is always "Because we have heard about or read about or seen pictures of it being done."

Then Ronn asks, "Do you believe you can do it?" Most people immediately have difficulty believing they can do it. They may believe that it can be done, but not necessarily that they can do it. Some participants may think that maybe they can do it, but they don't really know. Why? Because they haven't actually done it. They have not experienced it, so they don't know for sure.

## Development of Your Beliefs

You see, your belief system is most often based upon what you have experienced. Not what others have experienced. Your limitations are based upon what you believe you are capable of doing. And what you believe you are capable of doing is limited by what you have done in the past (your experiences). So you may think that you are capable of doing something, but you really don't know that you can do it because you have not actually done it. After you have done it a few times, then you start to believe that you can do it. But if you have alternately failed a few times in that activity, you have doubt as to whether you can do it all the time. And so on.

Can you see how important this concept is for an athlete? Can you see how important this concept is for a race driver at any level? The question then becomes "Which comes first, the chicken or the egg?" Which comes first, the ability to drive fast or the belief that you can drive fast? The quickness or the belief that you are quick? The winning or the belief that you are a winner? The losing or the belief that you are a loser?

Our experience of a prior result, a situation, a specific race track, etc., will begin to form the programming toward a personal belief system. It is very interesting to look at the tendency of some drivers' performances at the same track or event over the years. For example, for years Al Unser Jr. practically owned the Long Beach CART race. Can you imagine what his belief system was saying each year he went back there?

Your belief system can be the result of positive as well as negative experiences. You can gain confidence in your ability to handle a specific situation or condition as the result of your successful experience. You can also lose confidence in your abilities as the result of unsuccessful experiences, or failures. And the more traumatic the experience, especially when pain, injury, or embarrassment are associated with the experience, the more effective the programming. Of course, it is also true that the more joy and fun that you have from an experience, the more effective the programming.

Yet, as human beings, we tend to learn from our mistakes. We might draw the conclusion, then, that as we are making our mistakes, we are programming the mistakes (the wrong things). This conclusion would be accurate if we did not learn to make changes, to learn what not to do and determine what we can do that will make a change.

Most of us have experienced happenings in our lives that have created major impacts upon our perceptions; especially the programming that is the cause for the way we look at ourselves. These positive or negative happenings can form long-lasting parts of your belief system.

Ronn recalls the profound effect that a special teacher had on him during college. "She had three doctorates and one master's degree from various universities in Europe. Her husband was also a professor at Princeton. She was a brilliant woman, and one of the strongest personalities I had ever seen. I was raised in a small town in Oklahoma, and somehow wound up in college in Princeton—I had not even been east of Oklahoma before going to college. I had never met anyone like this woman, and I was totally in awe of her. One day after class, she pulled me aside and told me of the potential she thought I had, and of the high energy in my personality; how she could sense very special qualities, and what I could do with my life. I have never forgotten the way I felt after that. Although I didn't realize it at the time, she had a tremendous influence on my belief system—something I can feel to this day."

Many people have had experiences that have had the totally opposite effect. We have instructed a number of people who had made a decision not to drive 15 or more years before, as a result of harsh and critical parents and spouses who told them that they were terrible drivers, and would never be good drivers. They bought into it, and the event became a part of their belief system.

These types of events can create programming that can help you, and they can create limitations that can become almost impossible to overcome, unless you understand the process and know how to change the programming.

There is also a kind of confidence (belief system) that comes about as the result of knowledge. If you have broad-based knowledge in regard to what you are doing, if you really know what happens when you make specific changes to the suspension setup, or if you believe that your engineer knows what he is doing, etc., you have a tendency to have more confidence. Knowledge has a way of helping to break through limitation barriers. Doubt (lack of confidence) has a way of exponentially expanding limitations.

Knowledge is a critical part of your overall belief system, because you can't fool yourself. You can attempt to fool others, but there is one potential problem: You don't know what you don't know! If you don't know a lot, and don't know that you don't know much, you can get into serious trouble because of your naiveté. This is what a false sense of confidence is all about. Some people would say this is over confidence, but we believe that *false* confidence is more accurate.

We have all read books and heard lessons in all types of formats with the basic approach that you are what you think and what you believe—the power of positive thinking. And most of us can accept the basic truth (philosophically) of a self-fulfilling prophecy. But if you are to focus upon performance strategies, you need to do more than just agree that your belief system is important.

It seems that most of us are superstitious to some degree. We tend to perceive that luck, good or bad, is a result of some type of mystical alignment of energies that affects what happens to us; and, that we can maybe effect a change in this alignment to good luck if we wear the same pair of underwear under a driving suit, or we put a special stuffed animal in the seat of the car, or, as in the movie *Bull Durham*, we touch our bat with a voodoo doll for good luck, etc. Conversely, we will have bad luck if we don't have our lucky hat to wear, or don't have the ring given to us by our grandfather when we won our first race, etc.

Understand that superstition is an effect. The cause is our belief system. If you believe, really believe, that your ability to win a race is impacted by not having your lucky underwear, it will be almost impossible to win. Because at the subconscious level (in addition to consciously focusing upon not having your lucky underwear), your mind is not congruent with being able to win.

When you look at superstition from this perspective, you can realize that the superstition effect is absolutely valid. But rather than being something that is mystical, and totally dependent upon the alignment of the planets, it is the impact upon your belief system that (very objectively) makes a difference in your capability and the resulting performance.

As we discussed in chapter 5, when you use mental imagery, the mind accepts that you have, in fact, done what you imagined. You have actually experienced this result, this level of performance under the greatest pressure, this qualifying time, this consistency, this ability to maintain focus, etc. As a result of experiencing this mental equivalent in your mind, many times, over and over, with many successful repetitions, the representation of this situation or circumstance can be programmed (or de-programmed and reprogrammed) into your being. It becomes a part of you, your belief system about you and what you will (as opposed to what you can) do in a specific situation.

The power of your belief system is the power of your mental image of yourself and your abilities. And as you learn to program your belief system, you will learn to induce the performance level that you desire.

People have an infinite number and combination of very complex, multidimensional pieces of programming of their personal belief systems. Some people believe that they just aren't very coordinated. Some believe they are not good at qualifying. Some believe that they aren't good under pressure, while others thrive under pressure. Some people don't function well unless they are under pressure.

What about your belief system? What do you think needs to be changed? At the end of this chapter, we are going to ask you to define your beliefs. You will probably find this a difficult, time-consuming exercise. But, we think you will find it interesting! In order for you to change your belief system you must define specific areas, especially about driving a race car. You may find that other areas of your life impact your driving beliefs.

So, you are what you believe you are. What kind of a driver are you? Are you good in the rain? Are you good at qualifying? Are you good at the start of the race? Are you quicker when you are chasing someone? What does your belief system say about your racing abilities?

## INNER SPEED SECRET #16

### You can only do what you believe you can do.

### Strategies

You cannot *not* believe something in your belief system—it is part of your subconscious, your programming. But, through programming (mental imagery and effective practice) you can begin to change your belief system, by de-programming, programming, and reprogramming.

| Beliefs | |
|---|---|
| Positive | Negative |
| I'm great at race starts | I'm not a good qualifier |
| I'm a good, smart racer | I'm too nice a guy |
| I'm fast | I'm not confident enough |
| I'm assertive | I crash too often |
| I make good passes | I'm too tense in the car |
| I motivate my team | ... |

*Your list of beliefs may look something like this.*

Take a few moments to write down some of your beliefs, both positive and negative. Take a piece of paper and draw a line down the middle from top to bottom, forming two columns. Title one column *Positive Beliefs,* and the other *Negative Beliefs.* Then begin listing what you believe about yourself and your abilities as a race driver.

Obviously, being 100 percent honest is critical. If you try to fool your subconscious by writing down something that is not really true to you, the whole process will fail. The goal is to strengthen your strengths, and change your negatives to positives. That is why this will take some time. In fact, the more time you spend, the greater the impact. And no, you don't have to let anyone see your list.

Using mental imagery de-program, program and reprogram your beliefs. After doing this, and throughout the race season, it is a good idea to update your list of beliefs, and note how they have changed through the programming.

If you act as if you are someone, you will increase your chances of performing like that person. If you mimic or act as if you are Michael Schumacher, for example, both in and out of the race car, it will begin to program your belief system, and you will be more likely to drive the race car like him. Again, your belief system is programmable.

## INNER SPEED SECRET #17

### Act like who, or the way,
### you want to be.

A few years ago Ronn was working with a Formula Atlantic driver at a street race. "On the warm-up lap the car's clutch started to slip, so the driver pulled into the pit lane for an adjustment. So, he now had to start the race from the pit lane, behind 40 other Formula Atlantic cars. I ran to his car and asked him who he would want to drive his car in this situation. He had to be quick, and yet he had to be under control. The driver said 'Alain Prost.' I said, 'Then let Prost drive the car for the entire race.' With the help of some full-course yellow periods, he finished sixth, and had an absolute ball! He had acted as if he were Prost, and that affected his beliefs in a positive way."

# Chapter 10

# State of Mind

A person's state of mind can involve many things: the way he feels, attitude, fatigue, fear, confidence, anxiety, comfort level, anger, personality or behavioral traits, emotional condition, focus and concentration, stressful situations, problems in the family, etc. Frequently, several of these situations are interrelated.

*Emotion is a lovely privilege, but it is one I cannot afford during a race. If another driver has a shunt in front of me I must take advantage of any situation that may arise. I am, as I say, completely detached.*

**—Jackie Stewart**

Most states happen without conscious direction. That is, we don't often go into a state of mind as the result of our own conscious intent. Most of us don't define a specific state as an objective, much less have a strategy to trigger the desired state. We see something, feel something, do something, hear something, smell something, and we go into a state. We don't even know why we are feeling a certain mood or emotion. However, we can exercise more control over our state of mind if we have more awareness of the process and practice appropriate strategies.

Your state of mind is often triggered by prior experiences. It is important for you to have an understanding of how to program the triggers and anchors so that you are able to exercise more control over your state. And as a result, you can actually learn to induce a performance state of mind.

*A driver cannot allow his feelings to show. I plug my brain into the car and go on automatic pilot.*

**—Nigel Mansel**

Your state of mind actually has a functional, physiological impact upon your body. Your brain communicates to your muscles through bioelectrical energy. Emotions such as fear, anxiety, anger, etc., actually decrease the level of bioelectrical energy and therefore decrease the communication from the brain to the muscles. A rheostat on a dining room light fixture makes an excellent metaphor. If you turn down the rheostat, the light dims because the electrical energy going to the light decreases. Your state of mind does much the same. It acts like a rheostat between what your biocomputer directs your psychomotor skills to do, and what they actually do. State of mind affects brain integration by increasing or decreasing the flow of bioelectrical communication between the hemispheres of the brain.

In addition, the emotional response can cause you to contract muscles and hold your breath. We can separate the mental and the physical for discussion purposes, but functionally they are completely tied together—the mental state impacts the body. The bottom line is that negative emotions restrict the bioelectrical communication between your brain and body. If the muscles of your arms and shoulders are contracted, do you think you transmit more or less kinesthetic input to the brain? Do you think you have increased or decreased your ability to drive smoothly?

Some people seem to be an exception to this bad-state-of-mind rule. They actually perform at a higher level when under "pressure" and displaying anger. Tennis player John McEnroe seemed to be an exception to this rule. He performed at his best only after his anger had exploded. However, it only appears to be an exception. What actually occurred is that this anger had become his performance state of mind. When the tennis officials would not permit him to express this anger and disruption, he was not able to enter his performance state of mind. This state was programmed in him years earlier, and he had not developed a substitute performance state of mind, which limited his performance.

*Excitement is a racing driver's biggest problem. It can deteriorate a man's performance more than anything.*

**—Jackie Stewart**

Your state of mind will directly affect your ability to perform, and also the ability to learn. Driving a race car at any level is a high-energy, electric environment. At the highest levels, you can almost cut the electricity with a knife! You can literally feel the energy field! The resulting impact upon a driver's state of mind is seldom understood, and therefore, defining a strategy is usually not a part of the preparation process.

During the past several years, we have worked with athletes at all levels, including some at the highest level (Olympic, CART, and IRL drivers; European World Cup Soccer players; etc.) helping them to understand and implement strategies for better mental preparation to enhance their performance level. Athletes at this elite level have developed tremendous levels of psychomotor skills. Their biggest problem is performing at their highest level under heavy stress, which relates to what we would typically define as pressure.

In addition to affecting the bioelectrical communication, stress also triggers biochemical reactions in the brain. In our naiveté we sometimes think that it is good to "get the old adrenaline going," but in fact, that is not the objective. According to researchers, high levels of adrenaline can actually kill neurons in the brain areas used for thinking and memory. We can really get confused with trying to get psyched up. The net result is triggering all the effects of the fight or flight mechanism that we are born with, when that is not what we want. The objective, particularly under pressure, is to be relaxed and focused.

We have all heard athletes talk about their performance as a result of being tight, or relaxed, or being confident, or creating too much pressure for themselves, or being psyched out or psyched up, etc. These emotions play a critical role on their ability to perform at their potential.

Do you think that most drivers perform at their best, or their worst, in difficult driving conditions or high-pressure situations? While this is when the truly great drivers really shine, that is not the case for many. And although they may not perform at their worst, these drivers probably are not performing at their best. They may not have the confidence in their skill level to handle the worst conditions. And they don't have the strategies to perform at their highest level under the greatest pressure. We can all observe owners and team managers who have no concept of how to increase the driver's performance. In fact, we have observed many managers behave in a manner that causes exactly the opposite of what they want of their driver. Why? Because they don't know what to do. They don't understand the basic cause and effect of performance. So let's look at some strategies that you can use.

### Strategies

Understand how a negative state of mind can dis-integrate your mind; but remember, you cannot *not* feel pressure, tension, aggravation, anxiety, nervousness, stress, etc. You can, however, focus on positive states. When you feel negative, focus immediately and intensely on the feeling you had when you performed at your maximum in the past, or exactly what the car sounds or feels like when driving it. Trigger a positive state of mind program that you have developed.

## INNER SPEED SECRET #18

### Recall the feelings of your past successes.

For example, after reading this paragraph, put the book down and think about a negative experience from your past. It may or may not have been on the race track. It may have been an embarrassing social moment, a failure on an exam, a mistake at work, or a spin or crash on the track. See, hear, and feel yourself in that situation again. Spend about five minutes thinking about it.

*Recalling the images of past successes can help lead to future successes.*

Stop thinking about the situation, and notice how you feel. Do you feel *up* or *down*? Make note of your posture and your body temperature.

Now, after reading this paragraph, think about a very positive experience. It could be a race you won, something you did extremely well at work, helping a friend or relative, a personal relationship—anything positive. Again, spend five minutes just thinking about this experience.

Now, how do you feel? Up or down? Make note of your posture and body temperature again. Notice the difference?

Did you notice how simply thinking about different experiences can trigger a whole different state of mind, and what that did to your body? Understand the effect your state of mind can have on your performance, and how quickly you can turn a negative state into a positive one. Then, spend time building positive state of mind programs through mental imagery.

# Chapter 11

# *Personality Traits*

Psychologists, psychiatrists, and corporate personnel officers use a variety of tests to determine the personality or behavioral traits of a person, often to help judge the suitability of the individual for a particular job. With extensive training, personality profiling is an excellent tool to understand and define specific areas that may help the productivity of company personnel.

Although there are a number of different tests used, one of the most popular breaks down a person's personality into four categories:

**Dominance (D)**
The need for a person to be in control, or dominate, his or her environment. High D people are dominant people; at the bottom end of the scale (someone with a low D), domination is just not important.

**Extroversion (E)**
The need for a person to be around and communicate with other people. Some people have a high E—they are extroverted or out-going; others are introverted, and are not comfortable being around a lot of other people—low E.

**Pace/Patience (P)**
The need for a person to get something done quickly. At one end of the scale you have a high P—the person is able to patiently wait on something to happen; at the other end, the person is impatient and has a high sense of urgency—a low P.

**Conformity (C)**
The need for a person to do things with a great deal of accuracy and detail. A high C level means the person likes details; for low C people, the importance of detail may mean little.

All human beings display these traits in various degrees in their behavior. If we place each of these traits on a scale, and look at the degree of intensity of each trait, we can begin to understand that a lot of our behaviors in life are the result of the programming of these traits. Most of our life experiences, relationships, and a lot of mysterious, indefinable influences have impacted our personality profile.

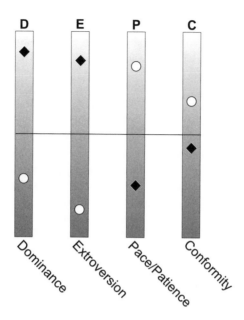

*The higher on the personality trait scale, the higher intensity of the trait. Here are two examples: The black diamond driver is a very dominant, extroverted person with little patience; his conformity level, or attention to detail, is middle of the road. The second, white circle driver is much less dominant, is introverted, patient, and is more likely to pay attention to detail.*

If a person has a high D, there is a strong need to be dominant or in charge of any situation. An extremely high D will be perceived by others as an absolute steamroller, and will interact with others based upon *telling* rather than *selling.* A low D will respond in a more passive manner, and it is not necessary for this person to take charge of the situation. The low D has a tendency to be less aggressive than a high D. This does not mean that a low D person cannot be a good leader. It just means that their leadership style will not be through aggressive behavior.

A high E will be very comfortable around a lot of people. While a low E will typically have fewer friends, their relationships with friends may be deeper. The high E enjoys talking, and it is very important to him to be liked by others. The low E doesn't enjoy talking in front of a group, and is less comfortable making a presentation to others—he is described as being shy.

A low P is very impatient, and wants everything to be done quickly, without wasting time. He has a very strong sense of urgency, and becomes frustrated when there is a delay in being able to get something done. The high P is patient, and accomplishes things with a much slower overall pace.

Conformity has to do with doing things by the book—and usually that is the "good" book or by the rules of the situation. The meaning of conformity has changed through usage over the years. We will look at it as having more to do with detail and thoroughness. If you wanted to hire a comptroller for your company, you would definitely want a high C. If you wanted to hire an engine builder, you would definitely want a high C. Detail is just not as important to the low C. To the low C, detail is like horseshoes—close is good enough.

The important thing to understand is that these behavioral traits are programmed deep into and become a part of your being. And for you to attempt to behave outside of your personal trait is very difficult. However, this does not mean that you can do nothing to change some of these influences. You are not just a robot, a sum total of prior personality programming. You can make a decision to be flexible, adapt and change to situations based upon the behavior required to handle a specific situation, rather than a reaction always based upon your belief system about your behavior. But it requires an understanding and a strategy.

The intensity of these traits and their relationship to one another, however, is where each individual is behaviorally unique. These trait relationships have a tremendous impact upon an individual's reaction to and the handling of a specific situation, especially under pressure and in highly intense or competitive situations. If a person is forced to function behaviorally in a way that is not comfortable to him, the anxiety will result in dis-integration, the contraction of muscles, decreased visual processing, burning a lot of mental energy—in other words, a reduction in performance level.

Just imagine a driver with a high dominance trait combined with a low patience trait, starting near the back of the pack. What kind of start do you think he will have? At what point do you think he will try to win the race? Or maybe we should ask, at what corner do you think he will crash?

And what do you think the odds are of a driver with a high P level winning a four-lap sprint car Trophy Dash? For endurance racing, would you want a driver with a high D and low P to understand the importance of race strategy at something more than an intellectual level? If you were a sponsor, would you want a high or low E level driver—an extrovert or introvert? And, where would you want a mechanic's C (attention to detail) level to be?

Over the past several years, we have conducted personality profiles with over 800 race drivers. Want to guess at what is the best profile for a race driver? Would it be a low D, or a high D, or a middle D? A low E or a high E? Should a driver have a low P or a high P? Think about this for a minute.

For different reasons, we might want a low D and a high D; a low P and a high P. We've observed that successful drivers have the ability to manage their *self*—the ability to dial each trait up or down based upon the situation. This is the driver who is not a robot, who continually reacts to situations by making good decisions, and can modify his *self*.

There are several drivers who are excellent examples of this, one way or the other. Rick Mears was one of the best examples of a driver who was able to manage himself, to be able to crank up the P for a while—becoming more patient—until the car could be balanced, and then crank down the P and go for the win.

Now, think about some current drivers, and what their personality traits would look like. Is Michael Schumacher patient or impatient (keeping it in relative terms to Formula One)? Sometimes he is, sometimes he's not. Is Dale Earnhardt an extrovert or introvert? Is he always dominant? How would you describe Michael Andretti?

So, what is the ultimate makeup of a champion race driver? There isn't one. Actually, the key is the ability to increase or decrease—to manage—your dominance, extroversion, pace/patience, or conformity level when necessary.

At one time, Dale Earnhardt was always aggressive (high D), impatient (low P), and introverted (low E). But one of the things that has made him the champion that he is, is the ability to manage his personality traits to his advantage. When his car is not as competitive as he would like, Earnhardt can be very patient—his finishing record is amazing. For someone who is basically a pretty shy (introverted) person, he can turn up his extrovert level when it comes time for a sponsor appearance or television interview. He hasn't always been that way. He has learned how to manage his personality traits. You can too—and you should.

The only way to do that is to have a program. You need to develop a program for being aggressive (dominant) when appropriate, or patient, or outgoing (extroverted)—whatever the situation dictates. At the start of a long race, you need to be patient. At the end, or in a short race, you may need to be more aggressive and less patient. Out of the race car, you may naturally be introverted, but when it comes time to wear the sponsor's hat, you need to crank up your extrovert level.

> *All a good tennis player needs is a pair*
> *of pumps and a racket. A good F1 driver needs*
> *£30 million worth of technology and*
> *a character that suits the marketing*
> *strategy of the sponsor.*

**—Martin Brundle**

If you have the line going into a corner, you need to crank up your D level to shut the door on a competitor, and other drivers must know that you will shut the door. If you are attempting a pass while coming into a turn and you do not yet have the line, you must have a low enough D and high enough P to give up the corner to your competitor. These decisions cannot be made as a part of a conscious level process. It must be programmed. We're sure you've seen some top-level drivers get themselves into situations in which hundreds of thousands of dollars have been wasted when they needed to be a little more patient or a little more aggressive.

*A driver's life has two parts. One is how he behaves in his car, the other is how he behaves out of it.*

—Colin Chapman

The bottom line is that you must be able to control your personality traits to fit whatever it takes to win. There are times you need to be selfish, other times a giving team player, times you must be assertive, other times patient, and so on. This cannot be done with conversation or threats. You cannot change your behavioral program with a conscious-level strategy. It must be done with the creation of what we call mini-programs for handling a variety of specific situations and conditions.

## INNER SPEED SECRET #19

### Adapt your personality to suit the situation.

It is important to have an awareness of the personality traits within any team, but due to the high stress nature of the sport, it is critical within a race team.

Imagine the difficulties in communications between various personality profiles. The high D may have little respect for the low D. The low E thinks that the high E talks too much. The low P wants to get things done right now, and anyone who wants to wait is just wasting time, The high C needs more information to make a decision, while the low C/low P wants to get on with it right now—forget the information. And imagine the difficulty in communication between a high P/high C engineer wanting more information from a low P/high E driver!

We have worked with several race teams while coaching drivers. This is one area that we believe will be considered more important in the very near future. You can look at the successful teams, the communications, mutual respect, and energy within the team, and understand how important this really is. The management of team dynamics is a critical component to success.

### Strategies

To create a series of these mini-programs, you need to use the same process that we discussed in chapter 5 on mental imagery. Put yourself onto the track in a specific racing situation, and see yourself enter a turn without having control of the line, and making the decision to back out and wait. Then, put yourself into the same situation but with control of the line, and shut the door on your competitor(s). Put yourself into a racing virtual reality in which you have just a few laps remaining, and you are to determine a strategy to make a pass based upon what the other driver is doing. See, hear, and feel yourself doing it.

If you believe that you have a high P (better yet, find the opportunity to undergo a personality trait test and find out where you really are), you need to create a mini-program to create a greater sense of urgency at the time you need it. If you have a very high D trait, and are very aggressive in most situations, you must create a mini-program to lower the D and wait to make a better decision.

Using mental imagery, program various personality traits to suit specific situations. Develop an assertive mode program, a patient mode program, an outgoing personable mode program, a dominant team leader mode program, a conforming team player mode program, and so on.

Practice dialing up or down your personality traits. For a set time (a day, an hour, or even just a few minutes), act as assertively as possible—obviously, within reason. (Please, no road rage or personal confrontations!) Then, for the same amount of time, act very patient and calm. Do the same with your extrovert/introvert scale. If you are a naturally introverted person, find situations in which you can act very outgoing; practice being extroverted. If you are already an outgoing person, at a social gathering or where there are many people around, practice being withdrawn, inner-focused, or introverted. Do the same thing mentally. Visualize adapting your personality appropriately to suit different situations.

If you can learn to implement this behavioral control in the race car, you can apply it to all parts of your life, and vice versa. You can then be in control of your response to any situation based upon what you want, rather than upon your robot programming.

Take every opportunity in your life to consider what personality trait will suit your present situation best and act that way—be that way.

# Chapter 12

# *Focus*

## Concentration

Most people who have been involved in athletic activities have a basic understanding of the importance of focus and concentration—it is critically important. The problem is that most of those who are either competing or involved in coaching or teaching have little understanding of what focus or concentration really means.

Think of focus and concentration as the information that is going into our biocomputer—the brain. Focus and concentration can come from every information source we have discussed earlier—our focus can be from sensory input: visual (what we are looking at); auditory (what we are listening to); and kinesthetic (what we are feeling). Focus can also be what we are thinking about.

As an example, if you are driving down a highway while thinking about a trip to Hawaii, and your mind has your body relaxing on a nice warm beach, your vehicle is operating on automatic pilot (assuming you have the appropriate software in your biocomputer). If there is any type of a problem or crisis situation, you are probably not going to be able to react appropriately. Your biocomputer is processing information about Hawaii, rather than how to deal with the problem.

Another example that often leads to a major problem is when a driver is focusing upon a situation that has made him angry: now the focus is upon the situation, muscles are contracted, and the ability of the driver to react appropriately is substantially reduced.

Many people have at some point in their lives been the driver of a skidding car. And when they were, most drivers recalled what we believe is the most confusing piece of advice anyone is ever taught: steer into the skid. Think about it. As your car is skidding, with your life—or at least your car's life—passing before your eyes, deciding which way the skid is and which way is into the skid is not easy. It may not be incorrect advice, but it certainly is confusing, and not very useful, advice.

Of the tens of thousands of drivers we have instructed in skid control techniques, everyone would fit into one of three groups. When trying to control a skidding vehicle, they either:

- Naturally steered in the correct direction and avoided a crash;
- Steered in the wrong direction (most likely confused by the steer into the skid advice) and crashed; or
- Panicked, did absolutely nothing (well, maybe screamed!), and crashed.

That means that about two-thirds of all drivers respond inappropriately in a skid situation. Believe us, it's true.

Visual focus is the key, however, to controlling a skid. How? Have you ever noticed how your car will go wherever you look, or focus your eyes? If you look to the left, you will automatically steer to the left. Look to the right, you will steer to the right. This has lead us to coin the term *potholism* to define this process.

What is *potholism*? If you are driving down a street and look at a pothole in the road surface, and continue to look at (focus on) the pothole, you will hit the pothole. While it may seem humorous at times, there is an objective reason for hitting the pothole. The brain is receiving repetitions of visual input of the pothole, and is processing that information. This literally tells your body, the muscles in your arms, to direct the car toward the pothole. And if you do not instruct the body to do something else, you will hit the pothole.

So, to control a skidding vehicle all you have to remember is look where you want to go. If you look where you want to go, or focus your eyes where you want the car to go, you will automatically steer into the skid. Simple as that. Well, almost. When faced with a stressful situation, your brain doesn't always respond the way you want it to, unless you have a program to handle the situation. What we are really saying is you have to program looking where you want to go. You have to practice focusing.

When driving on the street, practice focusing exactly where you want the car to be placed, and not focusing where you don't want the car placed. Then, when on the race track, focusing on the line through the corner, and not the run-offs or walls at the edge of the track should be easy—you'll be driving by program.

And focus is not just a visual thing; it is a mental thing. You can focus your thoughts, and your attention, as well as your vision. Focus can also be a result of your state of mind or belief system.

The specific subject of focus can be input at either the conscious or subconscious level. You can consciously choose to think about something, or you can react to a situation that actually triggers a response based upon your programming resulting from a prior experience. In other words, your focus can be the result of a traumatic experience. After all, as human beings, we learn more effectively through experiential learning than any other manner.

To demonstrate the impact and importance of what we actually choose to focus upon, we use a very low-tech tool that is very effective in increasing the awareness of the concept of focus.

Attach a washer or paper clip to a 6- to 8-inch piece of string. Hold the end of the string so that the washer on the other end is about 1 inch above the center of the circle on the next page. Visually look back and forth to alternating quadrant numers (such as 1 to 3 to 1 to 3, etc.; then change to 2 to 4 to 2 to 4, etc.) See what happens to the washer. It will probably begin to swing in the exact direction that you are looking. When you change from 1 to 3 to 2 to 4, you will see that it takes a period of time to adjust to the new direction that you are looking. Then, look slowly from 1 to 2 to 3 to 4 to 1 to 2 to 3 to 4 etc., and see what happens.

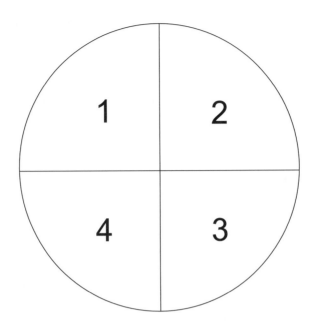

*This simple focus circle demonstration shows the power of your focus.*

*Note:* We have found that for approximately 20 to 25 percent of people doing this exercise, the washer will not move. This is because some people, when the washer just begins to move, will quickly and subconsciously, balance it with their hands so that it does not appear that they are moving the washer (which they are, of course).

If you focus (visual, thoughts, feelings, etc.) upon a problem, a past problem, a piece of concrete, what you or someone else is doing wrong, or what you are going to be doing tomorrow, the brain will process that information. The ability to see (mentally) a problem and automatically focus upon the solution is a trained (programmed) response. Sometimes it is easier to continue to focus upon the problem. It is not a conscious decision; it comes as the result of your programming. In most circumstances, especially while driving, there is simply not enough time to think about it. It is a reflex—a reaction!

This is why lectures about what to do are usually not very effective. A great teacher has the ability to get students to focus upon how to do it right, rather than what they are doing wrong. Remember, the brain cannot *not* think about something. If we say to the brain, "don't think about that wall," the brain cannot *not* think about the wall. What you can do is think about (focus on) the ideal line, rather than the wall. You can focus on what you want to do, rather than on what you don't want to do.

# INNER SPEED SECRET #20

## Focus on what you want, not what you don't want.

### Attention

Closely related to focus and concentration is attention. In fact, attention is the act of focusing your concentration (at some level of exclusion) upon something. The ability to maintain focus for a qualifying lap or two is critical. The ability to maintain focus while leading a race is critical. The ability to focus upon Turn 3 while approaching it, after making a mistake in Turn 2, is critical. If you are focused upon the mistake you just made, the mistake is being processed, rather than what you want to be processing. And to whatever degree, a major part of your brain's capability will be involved in that process.

We are interested in two types of attention when driving a race car:

*Broad Attention*—in which you are focused on, and aware of, everything around you—like all the cars around you; and

*Narrow Attention*—in which you are focused on one specific thing—like a reference point.

Driving a race car is a multidimensional, supercomplex activity requiring a unique level of multitasking abilities of the driver. As the level of racing goes higher, the complexity increases exponentially.

When driving a race car fast, on the track by yourself, you primarily rely on narrow attention. But to successfully race, you require both. You must be able to switch back and forth between broad and narrow attention very quickly, aware of the minute details of your line, reference points, and handling characteristics, as well as all other cars.

Relaxed concentration is essential to any high-performance endeavor, but especially to auto racing. It is important to be able to divide your attention between more than one object, thought, or activity at a time. In fact, driving a race car may involve splitting your attention between a multitude of things, all at the same time. You must be able to divide your attention appropriately between a variety of detailed elements (narrow attention), while always maintaining an awareness of the whole picture (broad attention).

At the same time, there is a limit to how much attention you can spend on any one particular thing at any one time. This is another one of the reasons why you must drive subconsciously. If you are having to consciously think about how to heel-and-toe, for example, you will not have enough attention available for more important things, such as how much traction is available, the line, and where other cars are around you. If you are making decisions at the conscious level, all other mental processing will be substantially slower.

It is important to have a quiet mind, especially at a time when concentration is mandatory. Multiple types or categories of information going into the brain will result in confusion and indecision; then comes chaos.

## Strategies

There are exercises you can do to improve your attention, focus, and concentration abilities.

### Narrow/Broad Attention

Focus all of your attention on one specific thing, such as a light switch on the wall, for 10 seconds—narrow attention. Then, while still looking at the light switch, broaden your attention to take in everything in the room (broad attention). Notice everything in your peripheral vision. Note all the sounds in the room. What does it feel like (temperature, air movement, the feeling of the surface of the chair you are sitting on, etc.)? Do this for 10 seconds. Then, back to the light switch (narrow attention). Alternate back and forth for 2 to 3 minutes. Then alternate back and forth between narrow and broad attention, but this time hold each for at least 15 seconds.

### Multitasking Attention

Practice dividing your attention by reading a book while listening to music. Focus fully on comprehending what you are reading and the words of the songs you are listening to. With practice you will be able to read very complex information and hear every word of the music you are listening to for a long period of time.

Next, sit in a chair and count just how many objects you can see, how many you can hear (and comprehend), and how many you can think about—all at the same time. Then pick just one of them, and focus on it. Then back to all of them. Notice, it is not just a visual thing. Be aware of, and focus your attention on not just what you can see, but also what you feel and hear.

While driving your car on the street, be aware of everything and everyone around you. Pay attention to the minute details of driving, and the big picture.

### Focused Concentration

Close your eyes and imagine a large 24-second clock, such as you would see on a basketball court. See the number "24" and hold it for a few seconds, excluding everything else from your mind. Then start a countdown as each second comes off: 23, 22, 21. . . .

If at any time you begin to think about something else—anything—stop and start over again. You will probably find this more difficult than you think. Now, close your eyes and look slightly up and take a full, deep breath. As you begin to exhale, see the number "3" flash into your mind three times; then the number "2" three times; and then the number "1" three times. This will tend to put you into a more relaxed, alpha wave–producing state.

Now, see the number "10" in your mind, and count down slowly—10, 9, 8, and continue down to 1. Take the time to breathe and exhale in small groups of numbers. As you count down each number, feel yourself going to a deeper level of relaxation. You are now at a deeper level of relaxation, and will be able to focus at a unique level of awareness.

Start the 24-second clock again and see how you do. If you practice this often, you will find that your ability to remain focused will increase substantially.

Finally, practice focusing while driving a track in your mind, and at the completion of each turn let go of the information as to how you did on that turn, and focus on the next turn. Drive several laps, and then "sit in your car" and feel how connected you are to the car, and how far in front of the car you are able to function.

# Chapter 13

# Decision Making

Making decisions in the race car is a very complex process, a result of both conscious and subconscious processing. In some activities, we have sufficient time to study all the available information, look at the various options, define the objectives, and make a decision. Even then, the wrong decision is sometimes made.

Most decisions made in a race car must be made in the twinkling of an eye—in a nanosecond. When the race car is at speed, especially in a contest for position, there is simply not enough time to gather all available information and make a weighted, informed decision. Things happen too fast. Decisions must be made quickly. The quality of a decision is based upon the quality of the programming. The quality of the programming is subject to a combination of many interrelated elements including behavioral or personality traits, prior traumatic experiences, states of mind, pressure, frustration, belief system, and a multitude of other elements.

We tend to perceive decision making as being done at the conscious level, and then wonder why we make the same stupid decisions time after time. Why? Because, given a similar set of circumstances, your decision-making database will have a tendency to reach the same conclusion—and you do it automatically.

When we observe a driver who consistently makes good decisions that lead to good results, we think of him as mature—he makes quality decisions based upon quality programming, which is the result of quality experiences. Or, we observe many talented young drivers who consistently make questionable decisions, and the driver or team manager tries to improve the quality of decisions by talking about it and making a decision that something needs to change. Eventually, some form of threat or punitive strategy is attempted, and almost always without success. In many cases, equipment is destroyed and thousands of dollars are wasted, without the lessons being learned.

This may be the greatest sin! Learning through our mistakes is at least one way to go through the learning process—if we learn and apply the lesson. If you don't, racing will become very expensive. Just ask some professional team owners.

Without understanding the process, and using an appropriate strategy to change the program, a driver will continue to make the same decisions—good or bad—because the racing environment does not allow the time to make deliberate decisions. So let's discuss the process, and ways we can make effective changes.

First, let's go back to the basics of the performance model. Information from various sources goes into the brain. The brain processes that information, like any other computer, based upon its software. Then you make a decision to do something—an action or reaction. The attempt to do this at the conscious level will result in confusion, sometimes indecision, and very often a mistake.

We need to understand that the mistake is an effect, not a cause. That is, the wrong decision (mistake) is not the cause of a crash, for example. The programming that was used to make the decision was the cause of the crash. Therefore, the solution is to change that part of the programming that made the decision.

Now let's talk about the elements of decisions. There are an infinite number of potential elements, but we will consider a few of the most important and their impact upon the decision-making process.

## Objective

Before you make a quality decision, you really need to have identified your primary objective for that activity. It is easy to identify a general objective in regard to qualifying, or winning a race, but that objective may change, based upon the situation.

## Motivation

What is the payoff? Is the payoff what I want? How close can I get to the payoff I want? A clear understanding of your motivation is a very important part of the decision-making process for you, and for your team. What if you are driving a car that is just not competitive at that moment? Have the objective and the motivation changed?

## Flexibility

Performance in all sports requires a certain amount of flexibility, because it is by its very nature a dynamic environment, constantly changing. Life itself requires a great deal of flexibility. The biggest problem most of us have is that our programming is set in concrete and we respond like a robot, no matter what changes in the situation may have occurred.

## Risk

What will you do and what won't you do to achieve the objective? Has the objective changed? If so, has the risk also changed? There is a critical balance of risk and reward that must be maintained while in the race car. It is totally different from taking a risk on a specific shot while playing tennis or "throwing a pass into double coverage." And the risk is not just your well-being, but the well-being of other drivers. The risk in a race car is considerable, which is a part of why we are choosing to play the game. But risk must also be managed, and must be a part of our decision-making process.

## Fight or Flight

This is important. As a race driver you have chosen to place yourself into a continual fight or flight situation. If you are not comfortable in that situation, if it is not fun, if it is not a kick, if your motivation is to prove something to someone else, or if your motivation is some other external reason, then stop doing it. Your brain does not want to be doing this, and you will trigger a fight or flight mechanism and make an inappropriate decision.

## Speed

The speed of the situation is one of the most important elements in the decision-making process, because the time factor will determine whether the decision will need to be made at the conscious or subconscious level. If there is plenty of time, the objective, changes, motivation, options, risk, etc., can be considered and weighed in the process. The race car at speed requires that most decisions be made at the subconscious level. There is simply not enough time to consider all of the elements and dimensions of the decision-making process. Most decisions will be made based upon the driver's "software."

Most people do not understand the difference in speed of processing between the conscious and subconscious levels. In fact, studies have shown that the conscious mind processes information at 2,000 bits per second (BPS); while the subconscious mind processes information at 4 billion BPS. That is why decisions in the race car must be made at the subconscious level.

Let's look at an example of complex decision making.

The strategy of decision making in tennis is interesting, even at the basic level. How are you going to return a shot and what are you going to do with it in preparation for the next shot or two? What do you want your opponent to do with his shot and how do you do that? At a high level of tennis, you don't have the time to make all of those decisions at the conscious level. A good tennis player must preprogram a specific strategy.

Strategy is not something that is just discussed, relying on conscious processing to execute the strategy. Assuming that the players both have the same level of skill, the tennis player who is executing a strategy that has been preprogrammed to the subconscious level (based upon the strengths and chinks in the opponent's game, and the strengths in his game) will win. The reason is that he is able to execute a strategy automatically, rather than just react to what is happening.

Most tennis played at the amateur level has absolutely no predefined strategy, and therefore most players are just reacting to whatever happens at that moment. The direction of the game is often in the hands of the opponent (although he is probably also running around reacting to what you are doing). But what if you had a strategy programmed? Would this give your game direction? You bet it would.

## Strategies

The only effective strategy to make a change in the quality of decisions is to deprogram and reprogram, making all of the most important elements of the decision-making process a part of your software or programming. In other words, you need to develop a comprehensive perception and consideration of many potential situations, based upon all elements and dimensions—essentially creating a multifaceted "what if" scenario for as many situations as can be imagined. But just "thinking" about it will not do anything. You must make them a part of your software, through mental programming.

Take the time to consider and define for yourself what your objectives are, what your motivation is, how flexible you are with each of these, and how much risk you are willing to accept.

## INNER SPEED SECRET #21
### Program your decisions.

The first thing to do is take an audit of past decisions that did not produce the result you desired. What are the typical problem areas, situations, behaviors, etc., that have resulted in bad decisions you have made? Actual, specific situations need to be written down with as much detail as possible. Then you need to think through each specific situation, weigh the information carefully, and determine *if* the decision was wrong, and why. Write everything down, and attempt to make the determination based upon logic and objectivity, rather than by justifying or rationalizing the prior decisions.

Look at all the decisions in relation to the elements we have discussed. See if you can define each element within a specific situation. What would have been a better strategy? What elements or part of your programming would you need to change to have made a better decision at that time? Make detailed notes about specific situations.

For example, there are 10 laps left in the race, your car is not handling very well, you are in sixth position, five seconds behind the car in fifth position and three seconds in front of the car in seventh position. Has your objective changed? Has your motivation and what you are willing to risk changed? Have you become more flexible?

Now, let's say that the car in fifth position has started to lose speed for whatever reason. Now what would you do? Can you go into a quicker mode that is half a second or so quicker, without placing the car and the position at a high level of risk? What condition are your tires in? Are you going to have to push too hard and overwork your tires? What would you do? Do you have a strategy?

The more scenarios you play out in your mind—the more preprogramming you do—the quicker and more appropriate your decisions will be. Making good decisions in a racing environment requires quality programming. Your performance will be more consistent, and you will achieve the desired results with a better decision-making strategy developed through mental programming.

# Chapter 14

# *Psychomotor Skills*

Psychomotor skill means that the brain (psycho) is directing the body (motor) to do a specific task or activity. Every athletic activity must become a psychomotor skill in order for the person to perform that activity at a high level of performance. What seems to be the simple activity of walking, for example, is actually a complex psychomotor skill, which requires a tremendously complicated program in order to walk at a subconscious level. If we consciously directed all the bones, muscles, and ligaments to walk—how far, in what order, etc.—we would not walk very well.

When we start to learn something, we have to operate at the conscious level because we do not have the programming in our brain yet. This is why we may stumble for a while. But as we repeat (practice) the activity, we are programming our software to operate at the subconscious level. This is why it is so important for an instructor/teacher/coach to be very aware of the student during the learning process. If the wrong things are practiced, the wrong things will be learned (programmed).

The objective of psychomotor activity in a race car is this: you observe, you feel, you think, you send some bioelectrical messages through your body to the muscles that input to the car's controls, and the car does exactly what you want it to do.

Colorado State University has developed a "biomedical signal processing device," which will interpret a person's thoughts, translate that information into a computer, and in turn tell a machine to do something. For instance, a paraplegic could think about going over to the table and a motorized wheelchair would take him there. Wouldn't it be fantastic to drive a race car with just your thoughts? Electrical paraphernalia would be wired from your brain to the in-car computer, which would direct the car's servo-motors to turn, brake, shift, and accelerate. No steering wheel. No brake or throttle pedals. Nothing but your thoughts in control of the car.

When we ask this question in a seminar or during one-on-one work with a race driver, most drivers say they wouldn't want to race like that. It wouldn't be real. It wouldn't be challenging. So, on second thought, maybe that wouldn't be so great. (By the way, Formula One Grand Prix racing was not far away from this scenario a few years ago, with all of its "driver aides.")

But think about it. This is essentially what you do now. The only difference is your arms and legs are the servo-motors that direct the car. It is your mind that receives the information, processes it, and then directs the muscles of your arms and legs.

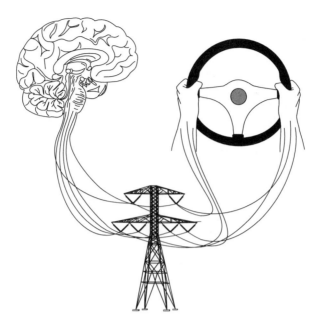

*Psychomotor skills—your brain transmits bioelectrical current to your muscles.*

Psychomotor skills are programmed into the subconscious by many repetitions. The brain produces a pattern of neurons, which becomes the identification to perform a specific activity. The result is an ability to drive at a subconscious level, while observing and making decisions at the conscious level. The programming is mostly a result of what you practice. If you practice the right things, the subconscious will recall exactly what you want to do. If you practice the wrong things, the subconscious will retrieve the wrong things. This is why strategies relative to practicing are so very important. And, this is why we often make the same mistakes, and it seems like déjà vu all over again!

For example, a young child learning to play the piano will spend hours practicing. This practice give the fingers the programming to function at a subconscious level. The problem is that repetitions of mistakes will program the mistakes—they will happen automatically. The parents and teacher of our young piano student at his first recital will know exactly when a mistake will occur—they've heard it practiced a thousand times. The mistake is now part of his program.

## INNER SPEED SECRET #22

### Practice the right skills.

Your level of psychomotor skill will always be a primary limitation to your performance. You cannot perform at a higher level than your skill. That is impossible. You simply do not have the software to perform at a higher level. However, through effective practice, you can increase your skill level.

When you consider all the complex maneuvers necessary to drive a race car at the very limit, it is an extremely sophisticated process. Once the sensory input of multiple, complicated, interrelated bits of information about the dynamic control of the race car is received by the brain, it must give orders to the muscles to execute specific actions, gather immediate feedback on how we are doing relative to where we want to go, process that information, give more orders to the muscles to execute new specific actions, gather more feedback, and so on.

The process itself demonstrates how fantastic the brain is. Everything is occurring in milliseconds—far too fast for this to be accomplished at a conscious or voluntary level. Performance in a race car is simply not a deliberate process. And the less deliberate, the quicker you will be. Unfortunately, many drivers attempt to drive a race car consciously. They get into the car and try to be quick. It just doesn't work that way.

Minimizing the number of cycles of sensory information input (processing information, orders for specific muscle responses, analysis of feedback processes) is the bottom line—the cause for quickness in a race car. This quickness is also totally subject to the bioelectrical quickness of the body's management system—the brain.

In the early stages of any psychomotor activity, we activate many more muscular movements than necessary. You can see this when we stumble through an unfamiliar activity. We are constantly obtaining feedback on how we are doing, and that feedback is essentially an error signal. After practicing to become more effective and efficient, we eliminate unnecessary movements. We become more precise and accurate. Elimination of unnecessary movements in any athletic activity is absolutely essential for increasing performance level.

Your performance, in fact, is limited by developing this more efficient movement. This is referred to by neurophysiologists as a *ballistic* movement. As the name suggests, a ballistic movement is like firing a gun. Once the trigger is pulled, the bullet will go exactly where it is aimed. That is, the information is stored in the brain as a chunk of instructions that can be executed in a single command.

The important thing about a ballistic movement is that it is very efficient. It is started by an initial electrical burst, which lasts just long enough to get the muscles moving at the right speed and in the right direction. The impulse is usually over by the time the muscle is halfway through its motion. This leaves the brain free to observe additional information that may require a change in the movement. Ballistic movements can occur in as few as 80 milliseconds, compared to a minimum of about 400 milliseconds for actions controlled by continuous feedback signals.

But, as a ballistic movement relies on only one signal, its trajectory, force, and speed have to be just right. Getting this movement to the subconscious level comes from practice, or repetitions of doing the right thing. This is why practice strategy is so critically important. Because the racing environment is dynamic (constantly changing) by nature, this allows the conscious mind to observe and process any new bits of information, and to direct the muscles of the body to make any necessary changes.

The role of practice is the same: to work out the best estimate of the initial ballistic input needed to put the race car on the course you desire, combined with the speed of the car (either under braking or acceleration).

You can then look at the performance of your psychomotor skills in terms of efficient memorizing and strategic forgetting. Efficient practice is a special kind of memorizing, based upon the most effective programming into the subconscious. Execution is a special kind of forgetting and elimination of unnecessary movement. That is, you must relinquish the illusion of moment-by-moment control, trusting the program to accomplish what needs to be done.

For example, you make the decision to pass someone under braking at the conscious thought level, but you must execute the braking technique at the subconscious level. Otherwise, two things will happen. First, most of your conscious attention will be spent on thinking about braking, leaving very little for observing everything else around you. And second, your execution of the braking technique will most likely be poor since it will not be automatic, and you will lock up the brakes.

At times, most of us have experienced being in the flow. It is effortless. It is a feeling of total connection. It is not accomplished by trying harder, or by willpower. In fact, trying harder usually creates anxiety, and that slows down the bioelectrical processing within the brain and the communication to the rest of the body. It also creates immediate changes in body chemistry, which substantially inhibit our ability to access our psychomotor skills. Using mental programming and effective physical practice is the key to your psychomotor skills becoming automatic and you maximizing your performance.

# Chapter 15

# The Care and Feeding
# of the Brain

## Nutrition

Almost everyone knows that what you eat has an effect on your body and your physical performance. What most people don't realize is just how much of an effect food has on your mental performance.

If you believe a particular food is not good for you, whether it is or not, your mental performance will suffer. A double whammy. Not only does it negatively affect you physically, it hurts you mentally. Why? Because, as you know, your belief system affects brain integration. If you believe a certain food you are eating is not good for you, your brain will begin to dis-integrate, and your performance will suffer.

In our Inner Speed Secrets seminar we perform muscle checks on participants so they become aware of the impact the food and drink they choose to put into their body during a race weekend has. Each participant experiences firsthand the impact on the mind and body of different food items through the use of a muscle check.

We perform a muscle check while participants hold some food they believe to be bad for them (perhaps some greasy bacon, potato chips, or a soft drink) in their hand. For most people, the arm will become weaker—the brain is switched off. Their performance potential has decreased. Why? Because your belief system believes these foods are bad for you, and whenever they are even in your mind, let alone your body, your brain becomes dis-integrated.

As you see, the importance of the *fueling* of the race driver is every bit as important as the octane of the fuel you choose to put into the race car. One would never consider putting a low-octane street fuel into a high-performance race car. Not only would it harm the inside of the engine (the way inappropriate food damages your body), it would severely limit the engine's performance (the way inappropriate food limits your brain).

Several books have been written in the past few years, some of which are excellent sources for what the body needs for good nutrition, especially the need for energy for athletic activities. Unfortunately there seem to be a lot of conflicting concepts, recommendations, and advice. As an example, several years ago a basic philosophy of eating healthy for everyone was built around pasta. Of course, the whole concept of carbo-loading came from being a good thing for athletes prior to endurance events, and therefore it was good for the

*If only you could refuel your body during pit stops, what you feed your body before races wouldn't be so important. But you can't!*

general public all the time. That was one theory. Now we have many more theories—nonfat diets, high-protein diets, high-carbohydrate diets, low-carbohydrate diets, blood-type diets, and so on.

The problem is that so much information has been published as fact that it is hard to know what to believe, and it is very hard to keep up with the newest and best dieting concept, especially since they are mostly designed as a way to reduce weight.

Your objective should be to look at what is the most appropriate sources of nutrition for the fueling of your body, and primary sources of energy for the brain. You need to look at the overall effect your diet has on your body chemistry, even as it relates to insulin. The balance and stability of insulin in the body is not just important for a diabetic, but is a critical ingredient in personal performance.

We do not claim to have the biochemical and nutritional expertise to recommend a specific personal diet for your body, but there are some recommendations that we will make relative to personal performance.

You are the only one who knows what is really the right diet for your body. Pay attention to what it tells you—not just what the food you are eating tastes like, but how you feel afterward. If you feel sluggish, unenergized and not mentally alert after a particular meal, make note. If you had just eaten a lot of red meat, or had a greasy hamburger and French fries, perhaps that is telling you what you should avoid—especially around race weekends. Of course, eating poorly between races will not be undone by two or three days of eating properly on a race weekend.

Once you discover what types of foods make you feel energized and mentally sharp, and which don't, you will probably begin to naturally crave the good food. After some time, your body will tell you what you need. Then you will begin to eat what you need, rather than just what you want. Just like driving, the key is becoming aware of what your body and mind really needs.

Eating a variety of foods (vegetables, fruits, legumes, grains, fish, poultry, meats), preferably fresh, unprocessed organically grown ones, will ensure you get the necessary combination of carbohydrates, proteins, and fats. But watch the way they are prepared. Zucchini may be a healthful vegetable, but not if it is battered and deep-fried!

Although there is no need for you to become an expert in dietary nutrition, it doesn't take much time and effort to gain a general, and valuable, understanding of what you need to perform at your maximum. Take the time to read the nutrition books recommended in Appendix C, and to monitor and respect what your body is telling you. And remember, it is just as important to know when and how to eat as it is to know what to eat.

Today, it is simply ignorant for a driver to rely on a candy bar as a source of quick energy for getting ready to perform an activity. The impact of a candy bar and a soft drink upon the body is swift and chaotic, causing immediate biochemical reactions in the body to handle the imbalance. The same is true of a greasy hamburger and French fries. It is almost ironic that one place that you most need to eat right—the race track—rarely offers anything but hamburgers and hot dogs.

Water is a critical ingredient for the function of the body. Many people today know the importance of drinking water, and yet many drivers do not prepare with enough hydration. This does not mean just taking a few gulps of water just before a race; it needs to be a strategy for the entire race weekend.

Water is the key to effectively conducting bioelectrical current from your brain to your body and back again. Just by drinking enough water, you will increase your concentration levels, you will be more physically coordinated, you will think more clearly, and you'll feel more energized. Also, researchers have discovered that anywhere from 1,000 to 10,000 times more oxygen binds to your blood when your body is fully hydrated. This reduces stress, helps remove waste and toxins from the body, and is essential for proper lymphatic function.

It is recommended that you drink at least one 10-ounce glass of water per day for every 30 pounds that you weigh; more if you are physically active (such as driving a race car or playing any sport). Add an extra glass for every cup of coffee or caffeinated soft drink you consume.

We doubt we really need to mention it to anyone serious enough to read this book, but we will anyway. The intake of alcohol severely impacts the hydration of the body. It dehydrates your body for a long time. Enough said. The decision is yours.

## INNER SPEED SECRET #23

### Your performance is limited by what you feed your mind and body.

## Breathing

We are all aware of the importance of breathing, as it relates to our survival. But most of us are not aware that breathing, or not breathing, is an absolutely critical factor in the level of our performance, especially in a crisis situation. Obviously, not breathing, after a period of time, will affect your body's need for oxygen. But long before that occurs, just holding your breath for a second or two or breathing in short, shallow breaths, communicates a message of anxiety to the brain that causes a dis-integration of the brain and a reduced flow of electrical energy to the rest of the body.

Although your brain is only about 2 percent of your total body weight, it uses approximately 20 percent of the oxygen going into your body.

In working with drivers, even at the highest level of the sport, very often we find that they hold their breath in a particularly difficult or dangerous section of a track. The moment that the breath is held, the information going into the brain is decreased, as well as the processing of that information in the brain. More time is required to send new information to the muscles, telling them how to respond to a situation.

Holding your breath will cause you to perform at a lower level at a time when you need to perform at your highest level. You need to program yourself to breathe in the car. Visualize yourself entering a high-speed corner. As you begin to turn the steering wheel, exhale slowly. Make the initial turn of the steering wheel a trigger for exhaling. See and feel yourself breathing deeply and slowly while driving the track. Believe it or not, breathing must become another program.

## INNER SPEED SECRET #24

### Program your breathing.

## Strategies

An excellent way of really understanding what happens psychologically and physiologically if you hold your breath is to have a muscle check performed on you. If you hold your breath while muscle checking, you will test weak—dis-integrated. When you take a full, deep breath, and let it out *very slowly* through your mouth, you should test strong, integrated.

Why? If you have done any weight lifting, you have no doubt heard from someone to exhale as you are lifting the weight. Many people think that the reason for this is to supply oxygen to your body. Actually, it has nothing to do with not having oxygen. (It might after a few seconds, but not at that instant!)

The reason is because of the representation (the programming in your subconscious) that holding your breath has. Basically, you hold your breath during two situations: (1) you are under water; or (2) you are experiencing fear. If you are holding your breath and the brain says "We're not under water," then it must be because of fear. Your brain will almost surely dis-integrate to some degree. For some people, there will be substantial dis-integration.

The point is that if you are breathing, the brain and body say, "Everything must be all right." If you hold your breath before lifting a weight that is near your maximum best lift, we guarantee that you will not be able to lift it. Your body will actually doubt your ability. In addition, if you hold your breath, there is an almost automatic response of tightening all muscles. This is also important to the race driver, because if you start contracting muscles, you are substantially decreasing the amount of kinesthetic input coming into your biocomputer—you are less sensitive to what the car is telling you.

Our Western culture has only recently begun to understand the importance of breathing. This may sound ridiculous, but it is true. It is true in birthing, relaxing, martial arts, and it is critical to your performance in a race car.

Breathing at any time must be done subconsciously. Amazingly, on the race track you may have to learn how to breathe subconsciously. Don't go out onto the track and try to breathe at specific points at a conscious level. As part of your mental imagery routine you need to preprogram exactly where you want to inhale and where you want to exhale on the track. Use the same mental imagery programming we've talked about to do this.

### Power Breathing

Power breathing is an exercise that you should practice three to five times every day, and more often on race weekends. It should be used as part of your preparation ritual immediately before getting into the car for practice, qualifying, or a race.

As we know, the performance of your brain is dependent upon the amount of oxygen that is delivered to it. Power breathing will help to put more oxygen into the blood, and the impact is very quick.

While sitting and relaxed (with your eyes closed if possible), inhale a full breath through your nostrils, for two seconds. Feel your belly fill with air as you inhale. When you have taken a full breath, hold it for eight counts (seconds). Then exhale through your mouth by letting your diaphragm press inward for four counts. Repeat 15 to 20 times.

# Chapter 16

# Learning

## Learning Styles

Not everyone learns in the same way. In fact, everyone learns differently. Some people's primary learning style is visual, meaning they learn most effectively by seeing things—visual processing. Others learn auditorily, by listening; while others learn mostly through experience or kinesthetically—through touch.

The important thing for you is to recognize what learning style is most effective for you. Do you learn best visually—by reading, watching, seeing things? Or do you understand things best when someone explains things to you—an auditory style? Or do things not really sink in or mean something to you until you actually experience it by touching it, feeling it, or doing it?

Unfortunately, many children are diagnosed as having learning deficiencies in school because of their preferred learning style. Think about when you were in school. Many things were taught auditorily, by a teacher lecturing, or visually, written on a blackboard or in a book. If a child learns almost entirely kinesthetically, he or she may lag behind others or be labeled "learning disabled."

Over the past number of years a lot of research has been conducted regarding learning by employing different teaching strategies. In all cases, the success of different groups being able to learn has been dependent upon the teaching style matching the learning style.

As you are learning a new technique, a new track, or just trying to shave off that last couple of tenths of a second, use your learning style effectively. If you are a visual learner, having someone tell you how to drive through a particular corner may be a frustrating experience, as you make very little progress. Have them draw you a picture. Or if you learn best kinesthetically, do everything you can to ride in a car with them.

Driving coaches need to be aware of their students' primary learning style. If it is visual, and the coach keeps talking about what they need to do, how effective will that be? Of course, the coach then would ask, "Why wasn't he listening? I told him what to do!"

Ultimately, you will use some of all the different learning styles in varying degrees, subject to specific activities. But you will usually have a primary or dominant style of learning. The most important thing to understand is that the effectiveness of the learning is limited by the dominant processing strategy used. Rather than just using your dominant strategy for a specific activity, such as driving a race car, research has shown that super-learning strategies use all styles at the same time. And, the more styles you use, the more effective the learning will be.

When you are using mental imagery, use your primary learning style, but use others as well. Imagine the sounds while driving the track. We know of a few drivers who actually take a small tape recorder in the car with them to record the sounds while driving around the track, and then replay it while actualizing. Concentrate on what you see—your visual input. And feel the dynamics of the car—the weight transfer, the tire slip, etc.—in your mind. If the smell of racing turns you on, you may even want to use the olfactory sense. Again, the more learning styles you use, the quicker you learn.

## INNER SPEED SECRET #25

### Know and use your preferred learning style.

### Learning Stages

Everyone goes through four stages when first learning an activity, whether riding a bike or driving a race car.

#### Unconscious Incompetence

We don't know what we don't know. For example, a baby who hasn't yet discovered that people can walk. This can also be the case with a race driver who doesn't know about a driving technique, such as left-foot braking.

#### Conscious Incompetence

We know what we don't know. The baby has now seen his parents walking, and wants to, but can't. Or a driver knows that a section of a track can be driven much quicker—he observes others going quicker—but he can't.

#### Conscious Competence

We know what we know—but we are having to do it at the conscious level. The child who is first learning to walk has to think about each and every step. The race driver knows what needs to be done, but he is still having to do it by thinking about it.

#### Unconscious Competence

We don't think about what we know. We know and we do—we don't have to think about it. The toddler no longer has to think about walking; it now happens automatically—he just does it! This is the stage that every driver must have as an objective for every track, in every possible condition, and for every potential handling state of the car.

Sound familiar? When you first began racing, you went through each stage with every new technique. As an example, look at the technique of heel-and-toe downshifting. Until someone told you about it, or you read about it, you didn't know it existed—stage one: *unconscious incompetence*. You then became aware of the technique, but didn't know how to do it—stage two: *conscious incompetence*. As you began to practice it, you had to think through each detail of heel-and-toeing—stage three: *conscious competence*. Finally, after practicing it over and over, it became automatic and you no longer had to think about it; you just did it—stage four: *unconscious competence*.

As you fine-tune and perfect techniques, you often go back to the *conscious competence* stage and then forward again to the *unconscious competence* stage, around and around through a loop. That's what learning and practicing is all about. However, some drivers have a difficult time moving from the *conscious* to the *unconscious competence* stage, thinking too much about what they are doing—it never becomes a program. Others operate only in the *unconscious competence* stage, and never improve. They never allow their conscious mind to observe, or see what could be done better.

For some reason, many people feel that knowing exactly how you do something may actually interfere with their ability to do it. In other words, they think

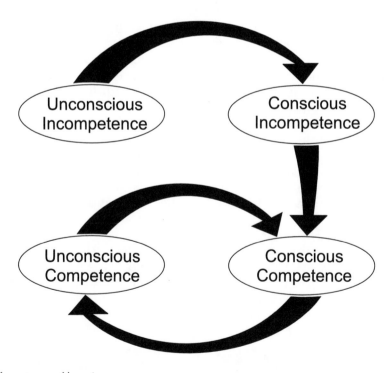

*The four stages of learning.*

that being unaware is necessary to doing something well—that knowing what you are doing will hinder your ability to do it. In reality, one difference between someone who performs well and a real superstar or master of the technique is that the master can explain how he does it. He is able to perform at the *unconscious competence* level while observing—while being *conscious* of what he is doing.

When you are really driving in the zone, it should be as if your conscious mind is the on-board television camera, observing everything that is going on, including your execution—but it doesn't interfere with your execution.

### Awareness

The key here is awareness. By simply being aware of what you are doing at the moment—aware of all the sensory inputs—you can accelerate the learning process. You can fast-forward the *conscious-unconscious-conscious-unconscious* loop. To learn, your brain requires two kinds of information: a clear mental picture of what you want to achieve, and good quality feedback—awareness. Without either one, your learning curve will be slow.

Think about it. You don't actually have to know how to do something to be able to do it. After all, you learned how to walk, run, and throw a ball without instruction, didn't you? All you need is a clear mental picture of what you want to accomplish, and then to be aware of all the physical sensations while trying it. Amazingly, your body will automatically figure out the best way of accomplishing the activity. Your brain will compare what you are doing with the mental image of what you want to be doing, and unconsciously make the necessary corrections.

In fact, by having a clear mental picture of what you want, and being deeply aware, you can practically skip the *conscious competence* stage altogether.

Let's use golf as an example. "Keep your eye on the ball" is probably the most dished-out piece of advice or instruction for driving the ball—as it should be, as watching the ball is the key to hitting the ball well. Or should it be? It seems that no matter how many times you hear that advice or tell yourself that, you still don't watch the ball connect with your club face as often as you should. Instead, what if you became very aware of the ball? What if the advice you received or gave yourself was to make note of the deformation of the ball as your club face strikes it? Or, what if you were asked to tell someone exactly where on the face of the club you hit the ball? By focusing on and being aware of the minute details, you will automatically watch the ball.

Same thing on the race track. Instead of consciously telling yourself to make the car run closer to the apex, simply make note of where you are—how close the car is to the apex. Just be aware—see and feel where the car is placed on the track—and you will unconsciously correct the car's path to match that of your mind's ideal image of the line. We'll look at this in more detail in chapter 17 when discussing self-coaching.

## INNER SPEED SECRET #26

### Be aware of what you are doing.

By the way, many drivers we have worked with, as their awareness level increases, actually begin to think their performance is getting worse. In fact, it is not. It is just that they have become more aware, more discerning of their techniques than ever before. If you reach that point, great! You are about to make a large step forward in your performance.

From this you can really understand why the quality and quantity of your sensory input (your awareness) and mental imagery are so critical.

## Copycat Learning

If you think about how you learned most things throughout your life, you realize just how important imitation and osmosis are as learning techniques. Through our combined driver training backgrounds, we've seen a dramatic correlation between the street driving abilities of new drivers and their parents. The better a driver the parents are, the better the new driver. Sixteen years or so of driver training while riding with your parents has a powerful impact.

Learn about, read about, watch, and study the really great race drivers. Just by closely observing them—becoming aware of what they do—you will begin to acquire some of their techniques and qualities. It is possible—in fact certain—that you will learn simply through osmosis and imitation.

Many people think the reason second-generation drivers such as Al Unser Jr. and Michael Andretti are so good is because they inherited talent from their respective fathers. While we won't argue the importance of good genes, we believe a major reason for their abilities has more to do with what they learned through osmosis—years of watching their fathers, talking and listening, picking up little bits of information and knowledge.

Tennis coaches in England, in fact, have reported a significant improvement in the performance of their students in the weeks following the television coverage of Wimbledon. Who says you can't learn something by watching TV?

Once you begin to study the greats and take on the style and techniques of the Schumachers, you will begin to develop your own style and technique. And yes, race driving involves style. Students of art always begin by copying the styles of the masters prior to developing their own style. The art of driving a race car is no different. If you act like Michael Schumacher, copy his style of driving, you are more likely to perform like him.

## Making Errors

Errors, or mistakes, are a natural part of learning anything. If you want to improve, don't resist them—learn from them. It is amazing what you can learn from your mistakes with a little bit of observation—awareness and thought.

Many people think that mistakes are bad, and a sign of not knowing how to do something—of even being an inadequate person. Unfortunately, parents and teachers instill that belief in many children. Many, even race drivers, never outgrow that belief.

The best race drivers in the world have made just as many errors as anyone else. The difference is they learn more from these errors, and they have discovered how to minimize the consequences of them. The key, again, is being aware of the problem. In fact, almost as soon as you have become aware of the problem, you will have corrected it.

One of the main differences between an experienced driver and an inexperienced one is the way they deal with errors. The experienced driver may make nearly as many mistakes. The difference is the experienced driver will correct, or minimize, the effects of most of them. And sometimes, he will also learn something from them that will help him to go even faster. The inexperienced driver, however, is not even aware of, let alone correcting, many errors until it is too late.

Trial and error is one of the most natural ways of learning; the error portion is just as important as the trial. Your first attempt at a technique is rarely perfect. It's usually a little bit off-base—an error. To some people, the error is then to be avoided at all costs—to the point of not even attempting it again. What a waste! Once you've made an attempt, your brain now has some feedback to work with to fine-tune the activity. Your next attempt, and each subsequent attempt, will be closer to your desired outcome, honing in on it. Learning is all about reducing errors to the point where they no longer affect the result.

Learning is much like an airplane in flight. Did you know that an airplane flying from North America to England is off-course 93 percent of the time? Its autopilot computers are constantly receiving input, recalculating, correcting, and sending new commands to the controls to alter the path. Your brain does much the same thing when you are learning.

In fact, it has been said that if you are not making mistakes, you are not really learning.

To learn from your mistakes, you must be aware of them and what caused them. You must acknowledge them. You must consider what you can do to improve. Then, you must clear them from your mind. Don't focus on them. Focus on the solution, the improvement, the corrections—how you will do it next time.

Many people talk about learning from their mistakes, but not as many actually do. It takes confidence in your own skills and abilities to learn from your errors, and learning from your errors builds confidence.

Speaking of confidence, when learning a technique or skill, break it down into simple, easy-to-manage steps. It's important throughout the learning process to experience some inspiring successes. Every little success leads to more confidence, which then leads to more success, more confidence, and so on.

## Strategies

Consider and define your personal preferred learning style. Do you learn best when someone verbally explains something to you? If so, you may be an auditory learner. Do you prefer to see or read what you are learning? Then you are primarily a visual learner. Or do you learn best with hands-on experience? If so, you are a kinesthetic learner. Think about a time when you picked up a subject or topic quickly. How was that taught? What about a time when you struggled in learning something. How was that taught?

Be aware of your learning style, and then use that information to your advantage when learning a new technique or a new track. Choose to have someone tell you about it, read or watch it, or just experience it by doing it. But also remember that developing other learning styles makes you more effective.

When learning any new technique, concept, or information, concentrate on being totally and completely aware of what and how you are doing throughout the activity, while you keep a mental picture of exactly what and how you want to be doing it.

# Chapter 17

# Coaching

Anytime you think about improving the way you do something, whether it's driving a race car, playing a musical instrument, or communicating with someone, you are coaching yourself. Self-coaching is, in fact, one of the most natural and important keys to improving your performance. And the key to self-coaching is awareness.

As we mentioned in the last chapter, being aware of exactly how you are performing an activity or technique is the first and most important step in improving your performance. So it only makes sense that the primary focus of self-coaching should be to make yourself aware of every intimate detail of what you and your car are doing.

How do you do that? By asking yourself questions—appropriate questions. You are attempting to do two things by asking yourself these questions.

The first is to dig deep, to discover the real root of the problem. Often, what you think is the problem is really just a symptom. For example, your car may understeer in the early part of a turn, and then switch to oversteer just after that. It's a common problem. You think you have two problems: early-corner understeer and mid- to late-corner oversteer. So, you make changes to the car to deal with each. With a little more digging, with some awareness-building questions, you may discover that your reaction to the early-corner understeer is to turn the steering wheel even more. Many drivers are unaware that they do this. Of course, with the steering wheel turned at a fairly extreme angle, once the car scrubs off some speed and the front tires get some grip, the car rotates quickly, causing oversteer. The oversteer is not the problem, it is a symptom.

The only way you are going to discover that is by digging deep with self-coaching questions.

The second reason for asking yourself awareness-building questions is that if you can become fully aware of what you are doing, and what is different from what you want to be doing, you will automatically—subconsciously—fix the problem. It is the most natural way of learning anything.

The first step is having a clear, well-defined picture of what you want to achieve, because if you don't know what you want, it's pretty difficult to get it. So, spend the time developing a full understanding and mental image of what you want. If you then become aware of what you're doing that does not match your goal, your subconscious will figure out a way of making the necessary improvements.

The key is to make your awareness observations positive, because your subconscious will work toward whatever it is you have in mind. If you become aware of something you are doing wrong, and have that negative image in your mind, your subconscious will work to get even closer to that image! If you notice instead what you need to do to improve, your brain will work toward that objective.

There is a world of difference between self-coaching and criticizing yourself, or beating yourself up. Criticizing yourself has the same effect as criticizing someone else. If done in a constructive way it can have a positive effect. If done in a destructive way, it will destroy your confidence, dis-integrate your mind, and greatly hinder your performance.

You want to become aware without being judgmental. You want to be positive. Instead of saying to yourself, "I'm braking too early for Turn 4" or "I always turn in early for Turn 6," change those observations into positive criticism, with positive images: "I'm going to brake later for Turn 4" and "I'm going to turn in later for Turn 6."

Instead of asking, "Why can't I take Turn 4 faster?" ask yourself, "What can I do to take Turn 4 faster?" or "What am I doing now?" or "Am I carrying too much speed into the corner?" The first question is destructive, the others are positive and constructive. "How," "what," "where," and "when" questions give you an understanding, an awareness, of what it is you are trying to achieve. "Why" questions may result in the reasons you are doing something, but they won't bring about a change. The focus should be upon the solution, rather than the problem.

## INNER SPEED SECRET #27

### Ask yourself positive, awareness-building questions.

Your goal should always be to improve your performance, while understanding that there will be some peaks and valleys—cycles of good and bad performances—to some extent, even if you follow every bit of advice in this book. Focus on the joy, the thrill of driving, the process rather than the outcome, and on being aware of what and how you are doing it. Expecting perfection is not only unrealistic, it will lessen your chances of performing well.

*Those who are too brave never make history because they don't know why they won when they win. A really good driver should always know why he has won and why he has lost.*

**—Juan Manuel Fangio**

*Continually ask yourself positive questions—self-coaching questions—to raise your awareness level.*

One other important aspect of self-coaching is accessing your beginner's mind. No matter how good you are, how successful you are, how many races you've won, you can always get better. The only time you stop improving is when you think you know it all.

Who learns quicker, a child or an adult? A child, right? In anything, you learn more at a faster pace when you are a beginner. The reason is, as a beginner, you have an open mind, no preconceived ideas. You are like a sponge, trying to soak up every bit of knowledge possible. Wouldn't it be wonderful if we could continue that way? Well, you can. Just open your mind and think of everything as a new and exciting adventure. Be childlike.

*To improve, and get better, is what I love—
and motor racing gives this to me.*

**—Ayrton Senna**

*Motor racing is an art, although not recognized as
such by the followers of ballet, music and so on.
Nevertheless, to me, to watch Fangio drifting
round a corner is as exhilarating as seeing a
Pavlova executing a graceful pirouette. Being
an art one can never finish learning. It may be
possible to reach the maximum speed round
a given corner in a given car, but there are
thousands of corners and many cars, as well as
varying surfaces and conditions. This impossibility
of reaching perfection gives one much scope for
improvement. I always feel that motor racing
is rather like chasing the rainbow's end, for the
more one learns or the nearer one gets to the end,
the further it draws away. It is this ever-
disappearing goal which one strives for that
makes it the most fascinating of all sports.*

**—Stirling Moss**

## Self-Coaching Questions

The following are just a few examples of awareness-building, self-coaching
questions:

- **Do I feel integrated, focused, ready?**
- Do I feel energized?
- Am I physically fit and ready? How about mentally ready?
- Am I driving subconsciously on autopilot?
- When approaching a corner, how far ahead am I looking?
- Just as I turn in to a corner, where am I looking?

- How quickly am I turning the steering wheel?
- Do I turn the steering wheel quickly in the initial part of the turn, and then slow down, or slowly at first and then speed up?
- Do I turn the steering wheel progressively?
- Am I unwinding the steering wheel from (at least) the apex on out?
- Am I letting the car run free out of the corner?
- Am I squeezing the brake pedal, or stomping on it?
- How quickly am I applying the throttle?
- Am I using the throttle like an on-off switch or squeezing and easing it?
- Is there anywhere where I could use full throttle—even for a fraction of a second?
- Am I apexing too early in Turn 1? Turn 2? Turn 3?
- Am I apexing too late in Turn 1? Turn 2? Turn 3?
- Am I aware of all the other cars around me?
- How does the car feel while braking? Is it stable?
- How does the car feel as I turn in to a corner?
- Can I delay my braking, instead continuing some braking into the corner? Will this help or hinder the turn-in?
- Is the steering responsive?
- Does it turn in crisply?
- Does it oversteer upon turn-in? Does it rotate too quickly?
- Does it understeer upon turn-in? Is that because the steering response is too slow—it doesn't turn in crisply?
- Does the car understeer or oversteer after the initial turn-in?
- Does the car feel like it rolls too much, or is it very flat and stiff?
- Does the understeer feel like a result of the car being too soft or too stiff? Does it feel like a big old Cadillac, or like a go-kart?
- Do the tires feel as if they are skating across the track surface, or is the car falling over?
- When the car oversteers, is it while I'm accelerating, or when I'm off throttle?
- What is the car doing—understeer or oversteer—in the first third of the corner? Second third of the corner? Last third?
- Does the car feel harsh or compliant over the bumps?
- On a scale of 1 to 10, how smooth was I that session?
- On a scale of 1 to 10, how was my personal performance that session/race/event?

## Coaches—the New Engineers

What is the one thing practically every sport has that auto racing has few of? The answer: coaches.

Isn't it odd that athletes in just about every other sport rely on coaches, and yet race drivers rarely do? Perhaps, if athletes in other sports need one to win, maybe you do. After all, driving a race car is an athletic endeavor. Michael Jordan had a coach he relied on so much he based part of his decision to retire on whether he could continue with him or not. Pete Sampras and Tiger Woods have coaches, as does every football, baseball, hockey, basketball, and soccer player.

So, why have race drivers typically not had coaches? First of all, we think it's because it's pretty easy for a race driver to blame any lack of results on his equipment, while a basketball or tennis player or golfer can't. Second, and this may be the biggest reason, having someone tell you how to drive fast is not very macho to some people. Third, coaching race driving is probably more difficult than most other sports, for the simple reason that the physical movements of the athlete are not as visible as they are in other sports. And last, since racing is so expensive, the extra cost of a coach, although relatively small, is seen as a waste.

To most people in racing, even some of the top team owners and managers, a driver either has the talent to make it, or he doesn't. Few understand just how much a driver can improve, especially with a little guidance. It is so easy for a driver to develop bad habits, and so difficult to be aware of them without a trained eye to observe and communicate them.

This may be changing, though. More and more drivers at all levels are discovering the benefits of having a coach. In fact, you may be surprised to find out just how many of the top drivers in the world—champions—have personal coaches. Of course, not all drivers will admit to having a coach, sometimes preferring to call them something else (manager, advisor, friend, helmet-carrier, etc.).

So, what exactly does a race driver coach do? A good one does a lot more than you would think. First, he determines where you need to go faster. But almost anyone can do that with a stopwatch and a track map. In fact, it takes a lot more than just determining where you are slower than the competition. It takes more than determining where you need to go faster. It even takes more than saying, "Brake later for Turn 1," for example, because *how* do you brake later for Turn 1? Unfortunately, that is exactly what many self-proclaimed coaches do.

A good coach will determine where you need to go faster, where you can go faster, what technique to use to go faster, what that technique involves, and exactly how to perform that technique—physically and mentally. The mental aspect is probably the most important. A good coach will help you become more aware and develop strategies to improve your performance, on and off the track. A good coach will guide you in all aspects that will further your career. In other words, he will do whatever is necessary to help you in going faster, winning more often, and making the best career decisions.

Does it work? From personal experience, we know it does. Taking into account the hundreds of drivers we've worked with over the past few years, the average improvement in lap time after just one day of at-track coaching is around one second. And most of these drivers have been very experienced and successful prior to us working with them. How much time, effort and money would you spend to make your car one second faster?

Of course, who the coach is makes a big difference. Having a coach is actually becoming a bit trendy in some series, such as the U.S. F2000 series, where many drivers have discovered that it takes a coach to win. Additionally, more and more experienced (and often underemployed) drivers are pronouncing themselves coaches. Some are very good. Some are not. Unfortunately, it's not easy to determine who's good and who's not. Looking at their coaching track record and checking references is the best place to start. Just because they work for, or have worked for, a racing school does not necessarily make them good. Just because they've won races themselves, does not necessarily make them good coaches.

Usually, a good coach has a broad racing experience himself. The more different types of cars and tracks he has driven, the better able he is to relate to the problems you're facing. But that isn't always the case. Just because the coach hasn't driven the same type of car you race, doesn't mean he may not be a good coach. We know some very good coaches who have very little racing experience. Technical knowledge, communication skills, an understanding of how the race driver's mind works, and knowing how and when to motivate are among the skills required of a good coach. The chemistry between driver and coach is critical. We've seen great coaches who were not able to help one particular driver, and yet worked wonders for others.

Communication, in fact, may just be the most important factor in a successful driver-coach relationship. No coach that we are aware of can read your mind. So you have to help him, tell him what works for you, what you want to work on, make him aware of your learning style, and help him know how to communicate with you. Do you want your coach to calm you down prior to a race? Do you want him to push you? Help you with your confidence? Give you a pep talk prior to a race, or leave you on your own?

It is in your own best interest to help your coach be as effective as possible with you. Take some of the responsibility to make it work.

Now, if a coach is not open to talking about your needs, if he doesn't understand your needs, if he doesn't believe in "all that mental stuff," if all he wants to do is tell you where you need to go faster, we think that tells you all you need to know about how effective a coach he will be. Look elsewhere.

As we said, having a coach is becoming more popular and acceptable. In fact, in the very near future, we believe that every professional race team will have one more full-time member—the driver engineer. And, just as the race car engineer's job is to get the maximum performance out of the race car, the driver engineer's role is to get the most out of the race driver.

A car engineer's role is to find and develop whatever it takes to make the car perform better. A driver engineer's role is to find and develop whatever it takes to make the driver perform better. That certainly includes coaching the driver. But it also includes managing the driver ouside of the car. That doesn't necessarily mean the driver engineer is the driver's manager, negotiating sponsor and team contracts, and other financial matters. It means making sure the driver is doing everything necessary to ensure his performance will be the best possile when in the car. It may mean developing strategies to improve the driver's physical fitness, ensuring the driver's personal life is enhancing his performance, and much more. And, definitely means developing strategies to improve the driver's mental fitness.

The driver engineer also works closely with the car engineer. In fact, often he is a liaison between the driver and car engineer, helping both the communication and the car development priorities. There are many times when a car engineer may , and does, make the car faster with some changes to it, but in doing so, the driver loses confidence in the car. In other words, the car is actually too fast for the driver's skill, confidence and experience levels. It may be that a more skilful and experienced driver could get into the car and make it go faster, but because the car is less forgiving our driver actually goes slower.

Of course, the feedback to the engineer is that the car is not as good, and the engineer then heads down a different (and less productive) direction with the car's development. Prior to that happening, the driver engineer must recognize the sit uation, and sit down with the car engineer and tell him that his change may be beyond the capabilities of the driver at that moment—give the driver more time before making that change. Other times, the driver engineer may suggest making a change to the car that will ultimately make the car slower, but will build the driver's confidence. Then, once the driver is confident, change the car back to the faster set-up.

Obviously, the driver engineer must be very good at "reading" the driver, just like a car engineer must be very good at "reading " data acquisition, driver feedback, and the appearance of the tires.

Ultimately, the driver engineer must be part teacher, part coach, part mentor, part psychologist, part car engineer, part data acquisition guy, part fitness trainer, part manager, part team mate, part friend, and part confidant.

Finally, two more questions to consider on the subject of coaching: How much money was spent last season on trying to make your race car faster? How much was spent on making you faster? If the answer to that last question was "not much," don't worry. You're not alone. However, if you really care about improving your race driving, consider a coach. It may just be the most cost-effective strategy for becoming a consistent winner.

# Chapter 18

# Skills and Techniques

In this chapter we will give an overview of the physical skills and techniques that a race driver requires to drive fast and win races. Instead of the typical technical discussion of the techniques, though, we will look at them strictly from the mental point of view.

## Traction Sensing

Traction sensing is the feel you get of how much traction you have to work with. It is the epitome of car control, which is the ability to control the car at the very limit of traction. Without finely developed traction-sensing abilities, you will never be able to drive the car at the limit with any consistency. Once you know how much traction you have, you can then alter your speed to maximize its use.

Traction sensing is the skill used to determine whether or not you're driving at the limit. And in fact, that is probably the most elusive aspect of driving a race car: how do you really know when you are driving right at the very limit?

Your sensitivity to how much traction your car has, and whether you have reached the limit or not, is dependent on how much awareness or attention you have to spend on the mechanics of driving the car. If you are spending even the

*It would be so much easier if we could just reach out and feel the traction available!*

slightest amount of awareness on a basic technique (heel-and-toe downshifting, for example), your level of sensitivity to traction and the limit will be lessened. If you have to think about anything other than whether you're at the limit or not, your traction sensing abilities will suffer. That is why the basic act and techniques of driving a race car must become a subconscious program—so that the majority of your awareness is applied to the all-important traction sensing.

Your traction sensing skills come primarily from your visual and kinesthetic senses, including your sense of balance or equilibrium. Your hearing can also play a role if you can hear the sound of the tires over the engine noises.

> *A driver's relationship with his car is something very sensitive. You must be feeling exactly what the car is feeling and constantly adapt yourself to the way the car is. It is like the car is an extension of your body.*
>
> **—Emerson Fittipaldi**

Along with making the basic driving techniques a programmed skill through physical and mental practice, the quality of the sensory input to the brain is an important factor in sensing traction. Therefore, all the sensory input exercises presented in chapter 7 are critical in improving your traction-sensing skills. However, just focusing on and being aware of the sensation of the tires rolling and gripping the road surface while driving your street car will significantly improve your traction-sensing ability.

## Speed Sensing

Being able to precisely and innately sense and determine the speed the car is going, and more important, the speed it needs to be going at any specific point on the track is critical. We don't mean being able to sense the speed in terms of a number, such as "the car needs to be going 83.4 miles per hour at the entrance to Turn 4." After all, what good would knowing the exact number be? You certainly cannot look at a speedometer while racing into a corner. That is why it has to be an innate, gut sense of speed. Where does this feel or sense come from?

### Visually

As you drive, the speed at which objects on and off the track enter and leave your field of vision gives you a sense of speed. Generally, the more experience you have, the more accurate your speed sensing abilities. But, the better the quality of visual information going into the brain, the more accurate your sense of speed.

### Timing

With experience, your internal clock begins to keep track of how long it takes to go from location to location to location, and compares it to previous and similar experiences. Obviously, this happens without your conscious thought. It is something you do naturally. If it takes even a fraction of a second less time to go from your turn-in point to apex, for example, your mind interprets that as traveling faster.

### Feel

The faster you drive, the higher the g-forces acting against your body. Your muscles, or more specifically, your proprioceptive sensors, send that information to your brain, where it is translated into your sense of speed.

### Experience

Your sense of speed also comes from the programming in your brain from past experiences. If, for example, you have applied the brakes with a certain level of pressure from X miles per hour for Y amount of time, your brain will program that experience, and recall it over and over again if desired, and even when not desired if allowed. This is why focused practice is so important. If you brake at varying levels of pressure during practice, not only will you have programmed inconsistent braking into your brain—leading to even more inconsistent braking—but your sense of speed will be less accurate. Of course,

*You must have an innate sense of the speed you are traveling, and how much it needs to be altered in preparation for each and every corner.*

an inaccurate sense of speed leads to even more inconsistent braking, meaning the whole cycle gets worse and worse, or at best, not improving. You see, again, why proper practice techniques are so critical.

All of this gets right back to how important the quality of sensory input is to your brain. Once again, by simply being aware of these factors when driving on the street, and improving your sensory input, your speed-sensing skills will improve.

## Directional Control

Even though your arms and hands actually turn the steering wheel, it is your vision that determines your direction. In fact, as we mentioned earlier, you will steer toward whatever you focus your eyes on. If you look to the right, you will steer to the right. If you look to the left, you will steer to the left. If you look at a spinning car on the track in front of you, you will steer toward it. If you look at the apex of a corner, you will steer toward it.

One of the secrets to driving on street circuits, ovals, or any track lined with cement walls is to *not* look at the walls. And that means mentally as well. Focus on the track—just the path or line you want the car to follow next to the wall. Do not even acknowledge the walls. There is only the path you want the car to follow.

Remember, you cannot *not* think about the walls. You can, and should, however, think about where you do want to go. Of course, you need to have a program for doing that. A program that tells your eyes and brain to focus on the track only.

*Look as far ahead as possible, and look where you want to go, not where you don't want to go.*

Before you can get somewhere, you need to know where it is you want to go. You must have a clear mental image of the path or line you want the car to follow through a corner prior to initiating the turn. In other words, you must know where you want the car to be placed at the exit of the corner as you begin to turn in to the corner. Without that, you will never be able to drive the car through a corner on the desired line.

## INNER SPEED SECRET #28

### What you see is where you go.

In fact, if you have a clear mental picture of where you want to be at the beginning of a corner and at the end, the middle of the corner will pretty much take care of itself.

*Once I have mastered the geography of the circuit the next stage follows naturally and usually quite quickly. This involves molding myself into the elements and consciously refusing to compete against them. Instead of looking for landmarks I synchronize my mental picture of the circuit with the picture that is being received by my eyes and I keep these two pictures in synch as I increase my speed.*

**—Jackie Stewart**

Obviously, eye-hand coordination is very important to driving a race car. And again, it's the quality and quantity of visual input to the brain that helps determine the quality of hand movement. As you may know, two of the first challenges that face a young baby are developing the neck muscles to the point where they can support the head, and developing the coordination to be able to reach out and grab something. Apparently, these two challenges are closely linked. A study has shown that when the heads of 5- to 8-week-old babies were supported upright, their ability to reach and grab things accurately was at the same level as 20-week-old babies. This suggests that the position and stability of your head plays a critical role in the accuracy of your hand movement, and therefore steering movement or directional control. Although the hands work under the guidance of the eyes, the head must be a dependable platform for the visual system. In other words, if you lean your head while cornering or if it is moving around a lot, possibly from weak neck muscles that cannot keep the head stable, the smoothness and accuracy of your steering movements will suffer.

This brings up two points. One, you must have strong, coordinated neck muscles. That comes from a proper exercise program, not just from driving. You will never be able to develop the necessary muscle strength and endurance simply from driving. It needs to be supplemented with an exercise program. And two, you must keep your head in as upright a position as possible while driving. If you lean your head, the information being sent to your brain will be skewed. Program your head position while driving on the street and at slow speeds on the race track (warm-up and cool-off laps), and while performing mental imagery.

As a demonstration of how important this is, make a light fist with your thumb up. Look at a spot and move your thumb to cover that spot. De-focus, and you should see two thumbs. Now tilt your head from one side to the other. You should see the two thumbs change in height relative to each other. This demonstrates that if you tilt your head to the side there is some visual distortion in spatial awareness.

When looking directly ahead, most people's visual field is approximately 180 degrees. This is divided into left, middle and right fields by your brain; each eye seeing about 120 degrees with an overlap of approximately 60 degrees. The information from the left eye is input directly into the right hemisphere of the brain, while information from the right eye goes into the left hemisphere. Information passing through the visual midline, especially in a dynamic environment, can be very confusing to the brain as to which hemisphere is supposed to be processing the information. This is one reason why integrated visual processing is

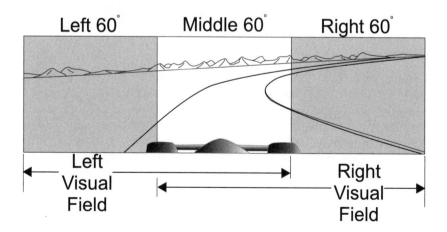

*Integrating your visual fields improves your overall view of the track and other competitors.*

so important. If your brain is not integrated, you will not see the whole picture. Is it important to have a clear picture of everything going on in front of you while driving a race car? You bet it is! Once again, brain integration plays a critical role in the accuracy of your directional control, so using the integration exercises presented in chapter 6 will help your vision.

## Manipulation of Controls

Your mental approach toward the physical use and manipulation of the controls (throttle, brakes, clutch, shifter/gearbox, steering wheel) plays a significant role in driving a race car. Many people, practically all wannabes, most novices, and many amateur and backmarker pros—feel that the faster they move the controls, the faster they will go. As anyone who has become successful at driving race cars will tell you, they are absolutely wrong.

*When I look fast, I'm not smooth and I am going slowly.*
*And when I look slow, I am smooth and going fast.*

—**Alain Prost**

The more precisely and gently you manipulate the controls, the faster you will be. *Economy of movement* should be the term that comes to mind when using the controls—not wanting to move them any more or faster than absolutely necessary to get the job done. Think finesse.

## INNER SPEED SECRET #29

### Smooth is fast.

As with practically every other skill mentioned in this chapter—and perhaps even more so with this technique—this can and should be practiced every time you get behind the wheel of your street car. Don't forget that whatever you practice while driving on the street is becoming programmed into your brain—good techniques and bad techniques. It only makes sense then to practice using the controls of your street car with finesse. Far too many race drivers underestimate the value and importance of street driving as a training and practice tool.

## Balancing the Car

One of the least thought-about, yet most important, techniques a race driver accomplishes when driving at or near the limit is balancing the car. Whenever you apply the brakes in a forward-moving car, the nose of the car dives, resulting from a dynamic transfer of weight. When you accelerate, weight transfers

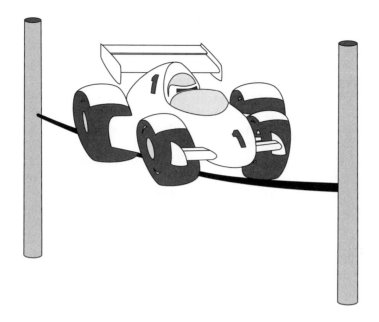

*Balancing the race car requires the skill of a tightrope walker—but at a much faster speed!*

rearward, causing the rear of the car to squat. When going around a corner, weight transfers toward the outside of the turn, causing the car to lean.

Without going into a long, detailed explanation (see *Speed Secrets* for more information), the less weight transfer that occurs, the more traction the car will have. The more traction, the later you can brake for corners, the faster you can drive through the corners, and the sooner you can accelerate out of corners. In other words, the better balanced you keep your car—the less weight transfer you cause—the faster you will be all around the racetrack.

Unfortunately, you cannot eliminate weight transfer. It's a fact of life—it's physics. However, you can minimize weight transfer, keeping the car as balanced as possible, by driving smoothly. As an example, imagine driving down a straightaway. When you get to a corner and turn the steering wheel, the car leans. Weight has transferred, and the car is less balanced than before turning. If you turned the steering wheel slowly and gently, though, the car will lean—the balance upset—less than if you quickly jerked the steering wheel into the corner. The same thing applies to how smoothly you use the brake and gas pedal. The smooth manipulation of the controls is so critical.

As you drive—even on the street—have a mental image of the car as a platform suspended at each corner by a spring (that's really what a car is), and try to keep the platform as level as possible at all times. If you work with this mental image all the time, you will naturally become more sensitive to the balance of the car.

Of course, your ability to balance the car is dictated by your own personal sense of balance. And, although your personal sense of balance is largely controlled by your inner ear, approximately 20 percent of the nerve fibers attached to your eyes are connected to the part of the brain that deals with balance. In other words, vision plays an important role in your sense of balance. So, the further ahead you look and the larger your field of vision is, the more accurate your sense of balance will be.

Any sport or activity (mountain biking, dirt biking, skiing, martial arts, tai chi, etc.) that requires a fine sense of balance will improve your race driving performance. The centering technique we presented in chapter 6 will also help your balance.

### Practice

As we discussed in the last chapter, having a qualified coach observe your driving, watching for bad techniques, and helping you become more aware, can be very valuable. Remember, practicing bad techniques is programming bad techniques, meaning you increase the chances of making them again. If you don't have a coach, you will have to use the self-coaching techniques we discussed, making yourself aware of what you are doing and making changes before any negative technique becomes programmed. This is also why your street driving technique is so critical.

Always remember, practice is programming, and you will race based upon those programs. You cannot drive in a practice or test session at 95 percent, and then expect to drive in the race at 100 percent. Practice with the same intensity level, the same focus, the state of mind, that you want in races.

Also, only practice for as long as you are performing well. If you begin to make errors, stop. There is no point in practicing errors. The old saying, "practice makes perfect" is wrong if you are practicing errors. Only perfect practice makes perfect.

## INNER SPEED SECRET #30

### Practice, at all times, the way you want to race.

The goal is to not make the same error more than twice. If you do, you are beginning to program the error. Making different errors is okay, as you are not giving them the chance to become a habit or program. In fact, making different errors sometimes helps you discover how a different approach can work. Practice is the time to try a variety of techniques, cornering lines, reference points, and so on.

That is not to suggest you should try to make errors on purpose. Remember, practice is all about programming what works and eliminating what doesn't.

Again, if you are making mistakes, especially the same ones over and over, stop. Review (become aware of) what you have been doing, get a clear mental picture of what you want to be doing, and then resume practice.

## Racecraft

There is a big difference between driving fast and racing. To win races you need to know how to drive fast, and to race you need racecraft. Racecraft is the art of passing, being passed, race strategy, and generally knowing where and when to position your car to improve your odds of qualifying well and winning races.

Your ultimate racecraft goal, then, is to minimize the amount of distance and speed lost when passing and being passed. Or, to maximize the distance and speed gained when dealing with your competitors. There really is an art to it.

Treating the other cars on the track, your competition, as simply changes in the track layout is an effective way of mentally approaching racecraft. When passing a competitor for example, rather than focusing on the car, think of the portion of the track he is running on as unusable. It is the same as if the track were narrower at that point, or oil was laid down there. It is then a very easy and relaxed act of simply placing your car on an alternate path or line to deal with it.

Use mental imagery to rehearse as many racecraft scenarios as possible. Play as many different variations of the start of a race as you can think of. See yourself passing and being passed, with and without lots of traffic around. Consider different options of how and where you can place your car so that it benefits you and impairs your competition. Use your imagination and play out as many strategies as possible.

Also, while watching races on television or at the track, put yourself in other drivers' positions and imagine how you would handle a passing situation. Watch how other drivers do it and try to figure out exactly why. Remember what we said about copycat learning in chapter 16. You can learn a lot about racecraft by watching others.

Ross grew up going to sprint car and supermodified races practically every weekend with his father. "I would sit in the stands watching how various drivers dealt with passing and being passed. Of course, in this type of racing on short ovals there were hundreds of position changes throughout the field in every race. I was fascinated how the real good drivers, the 'old pros,' were able to start at the back of the field and work their way to the front. I learned a lot about racecraft just watching those drivers—things I still use today."

Your racecraft will depend a lot upon your broad attention. The more aware you are of all the cars around you, the better your racecraft will be. Developing your broad attention is the key. This is one of the reasons drivers who have come from a karting background make such good race drivers. They have usually had years of experience being aware of competitors all around them—without the aid of mirrors. All the strategies designed to improve your broad attention will help your racecraft.

## Data Acquisition Sessions

Data acquisition systems are obviously very useful tools for helping set up and develop a race car. They are just as valuable as a driver development tool. A good engineer and a driver use data acquisition for the exact same reason: to become more aware. But where the engineer uses it to become more aware of what the car is doing, the driver can use it to become more aware of what he is doing.

Often, what you thought you were doing on the track is not really what you were doing at all, and the data acquisition system is good at identifying that. For example, many drivers who have gotten out of a race car claiming they took a particular high-speed turn at full throttle are amazed when the data acquisition shows they lifted slightly. Some drivers are doubtful and defensive as well. They claim the system must be wrong, and then stop using it altogether. What a waste.

Keep in mind, a data acquisition system is a tool. It is not out to prove you wrong and step on your ego. If you keep your mind open to what it can tell you, your performance will benefit.

Any situation in which you have the opportunity to compare data from another driver, whether in your car or another similar one, is extremely valuable. But you don't have to have someone else to compare to. You can compare with yourself, both with previous laps and sessions, as well as what you have mentally programmed.

It is a good idea to calibrate your awareness of what you are doing with what the data acquisition system is telling you. Once familiar with the system and what it can tell you, take a session to drive with a mental picture of what the data will look like. Then, after getting out of the car, compare your mental picture with the actual data. Soon, they will be almost identical. Of course, what this is doing is raising your awareness level and making it more accurate.

## Physical Exercises

It has been said many times—and not just in talking about race driving—that a physically fit body means a fit brain. Driving a race car is an athletic endeavor. If you are not physically up to the task of driving, you will not win. Obviously, you need the strength and endurance to physically handle the race car for at least the length of your longest race. But even if your body doesn't feel overly tired near the end of a race, it may actually be sapping mental energy away. By the time you begin to feel the odd ache or sore and tiring muscle, your concentration level has already begun to suffer.

## INNER SPEED SECRET #31

### *Physical exercise strengthens your mind.*

During a stress test for his heart and lungs, a doctor likened Emerson Fittipaldi's oxygen capacity to that of a 25-year-old Olympic marathon runner. Emerson was almost 50 years old at the time. As Fittipaldi says, "Motor car racing doesn't accept a mistake. And if your mind is clear, you'll be safer and perform better. We have a calculated risk in our sport. I love to be fit myself—not just for driving, but for my regular life. Everybody feels better when they're fit."

Practically every athlete in every other sport in the world spend some time prior to an event performing physical warm-ups. Very few race drivers do. The benefits of spending a few minutes physically warming up prior to getting in your car are many: improved blood flow; relaxed, energized, and more sensitive muscles; improved focus and concentration; and less cramping and sore muscles after the event. Use some of the physical movement exercises (cross crawls, lazy 8s, etc.) presented in the strategies sections throughout the book prior to getting behind the wheel.

Some of the best mental exercises you can do are physical exercises. Either on your own, or in conjunction with a physical trainer, and using some of the resources in the books listed in Appendix C, develop a regular physical training program. Then use it. It is your commitment to your training programs—mental and physical—that will make the biggest difference to your success in racing.

## Teamwork

Auto racing is an odd sport! At times, it is an individual sport, and at other times it is a team sport. It's an individual sport when you are on your own in the car competing against other drivers. But, without your team before, after, and often during the race, you will never win. How well you work with the team will dictate how well you do in racing.

In practically every case, the driver's role within a team is as team leader, whether stated or unstated. As team leader, you must learn to motivate everyone around you: mechanics, team owners, engineers, volunteers, etc.

Take Michael Schumacher for example. It's not simply a coincidence that the Benetton team became a winner while he was driving for them, and that Ferrari has followed suit. And it's not just his driving abilities, either. Everyone in both teams was motivated by Schumacher's personal commitment to doing whatever it takes to win. Ayrton Senna did the exact same thing with the teams he drove for.

Like Schumacher, you need to lead by example. The more commitment you demonstrate to them, the more willing they will be to match your efforts. The more effort you put into preparing physically and mentally, the more effort they will put into preparing your car. Your ability to motivate and lead your team may be more important than how much skill you have as a driver.

There is a long history of dynamic duos in racing—a teaming of a driver and his engineer/owner/chief mechanic who have combined to win more than their fair share of races. Jim Clark and Colin Chapman, Mario Andretti and Colin

Chapman, A.J. Foyt and George Bignotti, Niki Lauda and Ermanno Cuoghi, Michael Schumacher and Ross Brawn, Greg Moore and Steve Challis, Jeff Gordon and Ray Evernham. Some people have suggested that many of these drivers would never have achieved what they have without their partner. Most of these drivers would agree.

Of course, the basis for each of these successful partnerships is the same—communication. In each of these cases, the engineer/owner/chief mechanic knew exactly what the driver needed in and out of the car; and the driver knew what information the engineer/owner/chief mechanic needed and how to communicate it.

Communication within the team is vital—both ways. Yes, you must be able to communicate with your crew and engineer. But they must be able to communicate with you. The key is listening. Be open to ideas and suggestions your team makes, especially those that are aimed at making you a better driver.

Communicating to your engineer or mechanic what your car is doing is all about awareness. The important thing is to truthfully tell them exactly what you feel the car is doing. Many drivers think that they have to tell their crews something about the car, whether they actually feel anything or not—they make up, or exaggerate, what they think the car may be doing. Others, knowing what change has been made to the car, and what it should do in theory, will report something they may not have even experienced. Not all changes to race car setups respond the way theory says they should, and sometimes they make no difference whatsoever.

If you honestly don't feel a change to the car's setup has made a difference—or that it didn't respond the way you and the team thought it would—let them know. You'll be doing yourself and your team a big favor. It is always better to admit that you are not sure than it is to lead the team down the wrong path.

If you don't have the luxury of having an engineer or mechanic to help you identify what the car is doing, use the self-coaching questions presented in chapter 17. Ask yourself the appropriate questions to define exactly what and when the car is doing something, and what you are doing at that exact moment that may be causing that characteristic.

Establish right up front exactly what is expected of you by the team. If it's your team, you will probably set the guidelines. But if you have contracted a team or been fortunate enough to be hired by one, find out what the team owner and crew expect of you. Some teams want you around, others want you to get out of their way once you've gotten out of the car and debriefed with them. As long as you are not getting in the way, usually, spending time with the crew, observing, and lending the odd hand here and there can go a long way to building rapport and a relationship with the team.

As you have learned something about performance strategies for yourself, be willing to share thoughts and ideas with members of your team. However, be careful that you are sharing nuggets of wisdom rather than lecturing them on how much you know. As you learn more about personality traits, states of mind, and motivation of each member of your team, use that to build your team so that they are interested in their performance.

Learn how to read other people, how to motivate them, how to get your point across. Use every opportunity you can in your life to practice your communication skills. It may just make the difference between finishing first or second one day.

It is very interesting to observe the energy around a team, and how that energy impacts the performance of most of the team. We typically refer to that energy in terms of momentum, and through some sixth sense we can observe it and any change in it. It's not just what we see or hear, but our awareness of it is some special indefinable sense.

We can also observe the opposite of momentum when the performance of the team is in a downward spiral and becomes difficult to overcome. This negative momentum is very easy to observe in a team: Members of the team begin to find fault in what other members are doing and not doing. This energy, positive or negative, begins to rub off on other team members, the team stops working together, and the members begin to pull each other apart.

There can be an almost infinite number of reasons for that energy, and the change of that energy. But we typically look at that energy as a result of success or failure, rather than the cause of the success or failure. When things are going well, and everyone on the team seems to be pulling the oars together, and everyone feels really good about what they are doing and their contribution to the team, the momentum will continue until something changes it. Once the energy begins a downward spiral, however, it is very difficult to change the direction.

It is amazing how you can sense when a person with negative energy comes into a room, and how they can impact the energy of the room and every person in it. In our Inner Speed Secrets seminars with race drivers, we will ask one person to leave the room. While he is out of the room, we will set up a situation that the person knows nothing about. We instruct the people in the room to focus negative energy (think negatively about) toward the person when we say the number one, and to direct positive energy toward the person when we say the number two. We then ask the person to come back into the room, and prepare him for a muscle check. We say "one," wait a few seconds, and perform a muscle check. Without fail, the person will test weak, or switched off. Then we say "two," wait a few seconds, and check again. The person always checks strong and switched on.

We usually then repeat the process, asking the person if he can actually feel the difference. He can always feel a big difference in the muscle check, but has no idea why. In fact, the person typically has a very puzzled look because he doesn't know what is happening. When we explain it, it gets everyone's attention as to the effect of energy within a group of people.

We may not be able to explain momentum, or how this energy impacts others, but we can sure observe what happens. The negative energy of just one person in a closely related group, such as a race team, can infect the energy of the entire team. The negative energy of just one person is like a cancer within an organism. This is particularly important if the leadership of the team is contributing the negative energy.

For a team to be highly effective, each member of the team must maintain positive energy. We have found that the team can be more effective if each member understands the process, and the importance of his contribution to the energy and momentum. The leadership of a team, and that may be you whether stated or not, must be able to direct the team members toward this energy or spirit.

## INNER SPEED SECRET #32

### Build a winning team by example—lead the way.

One last thing. Your team doesn't have to like you, but it sure helps.

### Strategies
### Traction Sensing Sessions

Use a practice session (or at least part of it), or a test day to simply drive the car while being fully aware of the traction the car has. Use your vision to note the exact direction the car is traveling compared to the direction you have the steering wheel pointed. Listen to the sounds coming from the tires. Feel the slip between the tires and track surface, the vibrations, the g-forces. Notice the

The Lazy 8s exercise.

amount of roll or body lean the car has. Work at making the car slide more than usual and discover whether there is more or less traction. Also note how progressive the car and tires are—how much warning there is prior to the tires losing almost all their grip.

## Lazy 8s

Make a very light fist with the thumbnail pointing up. Bring the thumbnail in front of your nose with a slightly bent elbow. While focusing on the thumbnail, begin tracing a figure eight in a lying down position (called a lazy 8) with the hand at nose height and about shoulder width. Hold your head steady, and let your eyes track the thumbnail in the lazy 8 pattern. Continue with the exercise for about a minute or until your eyes and hand movement are completely smooth. (If you notice any jerking or uneven movement in the hand, or if your eyes do not want to stay on track, continue until they become fully integrated.) Then switch to the other hand. When that is smooth, clasp both hands together with the thumbs forming an X, and track the center of the X. As this becomes smooth, increase the pace of your hand movement gradually, until it becomes very fast, still tracking with the eyes. This exercise is also great for racket sports, baseball, etc.

As a variation, instead of focusing on your thumbnail, focus on a hole cut in a piece of cardboard. Take a piece of cardboard about 12 inches square and cut a 1-inch round hole in the middle. Hold the cardboard at the bottom corners, and then move it so that the hole follows a lazy 8 pattern. Focus your eyes on the background through the hole.

# Chapter 19

# Inner Race Driving

In this chapter, we will take a more so-called Eastern-world, philosophical, or attitudinal look at maximizing your performance. Very often, in our Western world's perceptions and left-brain training, it is easy to look at Eastern approaches as something that is voodoo and subjective. Once you understand and use these concepts, however, you will see they are actually factual and functional.

## Performance Revisited

By the very definition of the word *competitor*, we compete against others. However, if your focus is on competing, you lessen your chances of performing well. When you focus on your performance, you increase your chances of performing well, and therefore, of winning. Ironic, isn't it? Perhaps then, instead of *competitors*, we should consider ourselves *performers*.

Focus on your performance, your execution, rather than the result. Paradoxically, your best results will come when you are least concerned with them—when you focus on your performance. This may be one of the most difficult inner concepts to accept. After all, racing cars is all about competition—beating the competition. And yet, when you detach yourself from the results, you will reduce your stress level, become more relaxed, your brain integrated—you will be in the flow—and the results will take care of themselves.

If you think about it, you really can't control what your competition does, anyway. You have very little direct influence on them. All you can do is control your own performance. So, focus on what you can control, not what you can't.

## INNER SPEED SECRET #33

### Focus on your performance, and the results will look after themselves.

Research has actually shown that athletes focused on their own performance—their technique—have sharper vision and quicker reflexes than athletes focused on their results.

Don't worry about what other people say. Don't compare yourself to others. Compare yourself with your past performance, and strive to improve, no matter how you compare to the competition. Of all the drivers we've coached through the years, it's the ones who are constantly looking at and comparing themselves to their competition who struggle the most. The drivers who focus on themselves and don't worry about anyone else are the ones who win most often.

*Sometimes I try to beat other people's achievements but on many occasions I find it's better to beat my own achievements. That can give me more satisfaction. I don't feel happy if I am comfortable. It makes me go further and want to keep pushing.*

**—Ayrton Senna**

Only judge or evaluate yourself based upon what you've done—your performance—not on what other people say or think. Do what you think is right for you to achieve the goals you've set for yourself. Only you know what is right for you.

Winners focus on themselves today—in the present. They spend very little time, if any at all, looking at or talking about what they did or achieved in the past, or what they will do in the future. They look at the past only to learn from and improve. And yes, they have short and long-term goals, but they know it is today's performance that will enable them to achieve these goals.

It is when you are totally focused on the task at hand—in the present—and not on what has happened or will happen, that you most effectively activate your subconscious performance programs.

*You ignore everything and just concentrate. You forget about the rest of the world and become part of the car and track. It's a very special feeling—you're completely out of this world and completely into it. There's nothing like it.*

**—Jochen Rindt**

Expectations—thinking about a particular lap time, or a qualifying or race finish position—can really limit your performance. Often, with expectations, you are so focused on the outcome, the result, that it distracts you from the moment, from your technique—and ultimately, from your performance.

When you have no expectations, you have no limits, no preconceived ideas or thoughts to unfocus your mind. With expectations, you have pressure, stress, and anxiety that will negatively affect your performance. Plus, you will rarely ever exceed your expectations.

With many of the race drivers we coach, one of the first things we do is take the stopwatch right out of the equation. We have the driver just go out and drive, without thinking about or worrying about his lap times—his expectations. After all, why do you really care what your lap times are? If you turn a certain lap time, are you going to stop working at going even faster? We hope not! One of your objectives should be to *always* go faster.

*You must always believe you will become the best, but you must never believe you have done so.*

**—Juan Manuel Fangio**

Now, we know what you may be thinking: your lap times are a measurement, a comparison with your competition. The point is, though, you may be focusing too much on measuring and comparing yourself with the competition—the result. If you put that much focus and attention on your own performance you may be so far ahead of the competition that there will be no need to compare.

## Effort

As we said, one of your objectives should be to always go faster. Unfortunately, many drivers at that stage try to go faster. The result is rarely what the driver wants. Remember what we said about trying? Trying rarely works. Instead, don't force it. Relax, and just let it happen, focusing on your performance.

Either do something, or don't do something—there is no point in trying to do something. By the very definition of the word, trying gives you a way out, an excuse. Trying means "to attempt." To us, that doesn't sound very positive. It doesn't sound very positive to your brain either. Remember the muscle check. The second you try, you become tense. The second you become tense, your performance suffers.

As you know, driving a race car well—performing at your own 100 percent—comes from driving subconsciously. It comes from your program in your brain. Trying to drive fast is just like trying to make a computer with no software do something. It just isn't going to happen. Trying is driving consciously. Instead, focus on giving your biocomputer more input. Focus on what you can see, feel, and hear; become aware; and visualize the act of driving.

Have you ever noticed how practically every great athletic performance looks almost easy—effortless? Great performances, and therefore the best results, are always achieved when the right amount of effort is used in the right places. This right amount of effort is usually less than you think necessary. Like what we discussed in the chapter on psychomotor skills, the less unnecessary effort you spend, the more successful you will be. The key is to use appropriate effort—economy of movement.

Doing the wrong thing with more effort rarely results in a good performance. Great race drivers use less effort to produce great performances, and great results. The more intense the competition, the more they relax and just let it happen.

## INNER SPEED SECRET #34

### Relax, use less effort, and just let it happen.

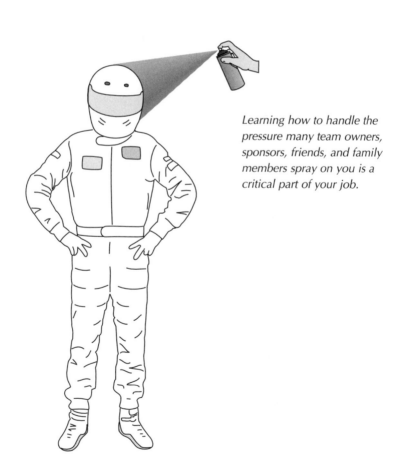

Learning how to handle the pressure many team owners, sponsors, friends, and family members spray on you is a critical part of your job.

Think back to some of your great performances in your life, whether in a sport or anything else. Were you tense, and aggressively trying—forcing yourself to perform well? Or, were you relaxed, calm, focused, assertive, and simply doing what seemed to come naturally? We bet you were in the latter mode, not even aware that you were trusting your subconscious programs to perform.

Again, focus on what you can control. Focus on what you want. Focus on where you want to go. Focus on the moment—your execution, your form, your technique—rather than on how much more there is to go, how much faster you need to go, or what position you are in.

## Pressure

One of the most frustrating things to observe is the pressure that is often placed on young athletes by the media. It's almost as if they go around with a can of pressure, and spray it all over the athletes. This is particularly seen in and around the Olympics. The media seem to love to remind Olympic athletes of past failures and mistakes, and ask them if they will be able to "put that out of their minds." If we really cared about the performances of our Olympic athletes, we would keep the media away from them. Of course, that's not going to happen.

The same is true of many race teams, and sometimes with the race media. If a team manager believes that he is enhancing the performance of the team and the driver by going around spraying little cans of pressure on everyone—especially the driver—perhaps the team manager needs to become more aware of the strategies that really will enhance performance.

For the race driver, having an understanding of pressure, and a strategy for controlling it, is critical.

Many drivers' performance level is limited by their fear of failing, their fear of losing. So much of their focus is upon not losing (again, an outcome), and what losing will mean (at least, what they think losing will mean), that they almost guarantee losing. It's unfortunate—not to mention, destructive—the amount of pressure, external and internal, some drivers put on themselves or have put on them from others.

Internal pressure, from yourself, is not necessarily a bad thing, as long as it is focused in the right direction. In fact, this sometimes helps to drive or motivate a person. But, most of the time, pressure to deliver an outcome only results in

*Pressure comes from within rather than from other people. And if pressure comes from other people it's how you deal with it. Pressure is something that builds when you're losing control.*

**—David Coulthard**

increased tension, stress and anxiety, and decreasing performance. Make sure any internal pressure you place on yourself is focused on your performance, not the result.

External pressure rarely, if ever, increases a driver's performance level, and most often leads to not winning. External pressure is the pressure a driver puts on himself to win in front of others, or to live up to others' expectations. It's also the pressure others, whether it is family, friends, sponsors, or crew members, put on the driver to win.

People who place this external pressure on their driver must realize how much they negatively affect the driver with their expectations. Understand that there is a difference between having and showing confidence in a driver, and having high expectations. Having confidence is a performance-related thing. High expectations are outcome related. Of course you know which is best.

*Pressure comes only when you have doubts about what you're doing, when you cannot see a way ahead. I do not worry about imponderables, about the word 'if.'*

**—Ayrton Senna**

The same thing applies to yourself. If you think about what people expect of you, what they will say about you, what their expectations are, you decrease your chances of winning. If you focus on your performance and forget about whether you may lose and the consequences of that, you increase your chances of winning.

## Positive Talk

Turn everything you can into a positive. For example, just by saying you love racing in the rain over and over again will make you a better driver in the rain. If you take every situation that other drivers consider a problem or unpleasant (rain, boring track, uncompetitive car, too much traffic, etc.) and turn them into positive challenges, you will perform better. Turn them into "watch this" situations—chances to tackle a challenge head-on and show what you can really do. It's simply a matter of turning negative thoughts and questions into positive talk.

A study showed that the average person has approximately 66,000 thoughts every day, with 70 to 80 percent of those being negative. We doubt that this study included any champion race drivers! From our observations, great race drivers seem to be able to turn almost everything into a positive. We would suggest that at least 70 to 80 percent of their thoughts are positive. (Some people might joke that race drivers are not capable of 66 thoughts per day—all of them about driving—let alone 66,000!)

The more times you repeat a phrase, the more it will become a part of your belief system. If you tell yourself over and over again that you are a great qualifier, eventually you will truly believe you are a great qualifier, and the greater your chances of being just that. It really is a self-fulfilling prophecy.

Early in Ross' career he spent a lot of time racing in the rain. "As I began racing against other drivers who hadn't had as much experience in the rain, I realized I had a slight advantage. But more importantly, the more I told myself I had an advantage in the rain, the more I really did. Of course, that resulted in some great performances in the rain, and therefore I enjoyed it even more. I still love to tell other drivers how much I love racing in the rain, and it still results in an advantage. I do the same with every thing that other drivers look at as problems. I love to make a point of letting other drivers know how much I enjoy and look forward to things they don't like. And when I am driving a car that is obviously uncompetitive, I look at that as an opportunity to really show off—to do more than anyone expected of me."

## Confidence

There is nothing that will build or improve your confidence like a little success. Fortunately, these successes do not necessarily have to be behind the wheel of a race car. Any success in anything will trigger your confidence level. So, focus on past successes. See them vividly in your mind's eye. Recall the emotions, the feelings, the performance you experienced with these successes.

Recall, using mental imagery, past successes you've had in other sports, in school, business, relationships, or hobbies. Replay every detail about those performances from a technique point of view, and how you felt, your emotions and your state of mind before, during, and after.

As we mentioned in the chapter on learning, confidence builds success and success builds confidence. It's a loop. The more confidence you have, the more likely you will have success. The more success you have, the more confidence you will have. Unfortunately, the opposite is also true!

Setting short-term and long-term goals—and achieving them—is important to your confidence. To do that, the goals must be realistic. Do not try to move up the racing career ladder too quickly. If you get behind the wheel of a race car that you are not mentally or physically ready for, it's very easy for you to lose confidence.

The same goes for something as simple as increasing your speed through a corner. If your immediate goal is to increase your speed through a turn by 2 miles per hour, that's achievable and helps build confidence so that you can improve even more. If your immediate goal is to increase your speed by 10 miles per hour, that may be too large a jump. If you don't succeed in making that jump, you may lose confidence and not make any further improvement.

*The first time is the most important because
you know you can do it again. You go
to every race after that thinking about
winning, not just taking part.*

**—Alain Prost**

Feed off your successes, no matter where and when they are in your life.

During the 1997 World Sports Car season, the average number of positions Ross improved during the first two laps was six. "The first race was the 12-hour at Sebring, where I qualified 10th. In the drivers meeting prior to the race, the officials said they had to start the race on time due to television coverage. During the pace lap, a car had a mechanical problem, which meant they had to run a second pace lap. Because of the TV time constraints, I knew right then that the green flag was going to fly at the end of that second pace lap, no matter what. So—let's just say I was in second place at the end of the first lap. Prior to the next race, I kept replaying that Sebring start over and over in my mind. I got another great start. In fact, for the rest of the season, I kept playing those race starts in my head—and kept getting great starts. I knew, prior to the start of every race, that I was going to pass at least four or five cars on the first lap. Replaying those successes in my head led to many more."

## INNER SPEED SECRET #35

### Replay your successes.

### Comfort Zone

Drivers usually operate within their comfort zones, going outside every once in a while to push the envelope. To go faster, to improve as a race driver, you have to have a comfort zone that extends beyond the limits of your car. In other words, if you are not comfortable driving as fast as the car can be driven, you will not be able to maximize your performance. If you're not comfortable driving slightly beyond the limits of your car every now and then (or at least your perception of the limits), you will never be able to consistently drive at the limit.

To improve your performance level, to stretch the limits of your comfort zone, you have to progressively push the limits in small increments. Some drivers never go beyond their comfort zone, and never improve. Others go too far too soon. If you take too big a leap, at best you won't improve! At worst a big crash.

You must feel completely comfortable and confident with the sense of speed just slightly beyond the limit. One of the best ways of doing that, although not always very practical, is to drive a car that is faster than the one you race. You then become so accustomed to a higher speed that when you return to the speed of your race car, it feels slow. The objective, really, is to help slow down the feeling of speed.

Short of spending time behind the wheel of a race car much faster than yours, mental imagery is the key to developing your comfort zone. As we said earlier, this can be done by driving a track in your mind, and then accelerating the speed in your mind to fast motion.

*It's easy to get too comfortable behind the wheel of the race car—and never push beyond your comfort zone. Of course, that will never lead to a great performance.*

## Intensity

Every time you get behind the wheel of a race car, you must perform at the same intensity level you want during a race. There is no point practicing in a casual, "I don't really care how I do this session—this session is not very important" attitude, and then expect to perform any differently in qualifying or the race. Remember, practice is programming. If you program driving with a low intensity level, that's how you'll perform in the heat of the battle.

*Speed? Really the whole process is the reverse*
*of speed, how to eliminate it. It doesn't exist*
*for me except when I am driving poorly.*
*Then things seem to be coming at me quickly*
*instead of passing in slow motion*
*and I know I'm off form.*

**—Jackie Stewart**

Particularly in some of the stepping-stone series, such as Formula 2000, Formula Atlantic, Indy Lights, Midgets, and the NASCAR regional tours, the competition is very intense—fierce, in fact. One technique we recommend to raise your intensity level is this: Every time you leave the pit lane, whether on a private test day, practice session, or qualifying, drive like you mean business. Accelerate hard out of the pits and get up to speed as quickly as possible. Push as hard as possible right away—be intense (but not tense!). This does not mean driving beyond your programming too soon and causing a problem.

If you slowly roll down pit lane and then gradually build up to speed, you may lose valuable time. Plus, and more important, it may take too long for you to mentally get up to speed—to dial up your intensity level. Quickly accelerating out of pit lane, being the first car out, driving as hard as possible right away, sets a tone for you and sends a message to your competition—you're here to do business. It is a trigger for your mental intensity.

Being intense often requires energizing yourself. Not being energized or intense is not a problem for many people in a sport such as racing, but still, it is not uncommon for drivers to be too calm, relaxed, or even fatigued. If that is you prior to practice, qualifying, or a race, you need a program for energizing. See yourself alive and energized. Then use some physical warm-up exercises (cross-crawls), clench your fists, flex your muscles, yell or scream, use powerful words when talking to people, get your heart rate pumping, take some deep rapid breaths, or listen to some loud rock music. As we have said, all drivers have specific and individual performance strategies. What works for you?

The same thing applies to your level of being psyched. Some drivers need to psych themselves up, while others must psych or calm themselves down. You need to determine what level of psyching results in your best performance. Each driver has his own optimum level of being psyched—the optimum level of emotions, tension, anxiety, nervousness, and energy. The key is to be aware of it at all times, and when it results in a superior or peak performance, to use that experience to program it so that you can recall it over and over again.

## Assertiveness Versus Aggressiveness

Traditional wisdom says that in any sport you must aggressively dominate your competition. Observe the great athletes: Michael Schumacher, Michael Jordan, Tiger Woods. They are not aggressive; they are assertive. It may seem to be a subtle difference in language—so subtle that many people use the word aggressive when they really mean assertive, and vice versa—but there is a significant difference between being aggressive and being assertive.

The dictionary defines assertion as "a behavior that emphasizes self-confidence and persistent determination to express oneself in a positive way." Aggressive, meanwhile "implies a bold, energetic pursuit of one's ends, connoting, in a derogatory usage, a ruthless desire to dominate, and in a favorable sense, enterprise, initiative, etc.; and rarely suggests the furthering of one's own ends."

Aggressive behavior is usually the result of a driver trying to hide something —a weakness. Your competitors will recognize that, and most likely take advantage of it.

An aggressive start is wild, not controlled, and often results in disaster. Being assertive means placing your car where you belong. It always appears in control, because it is.

## INNER SPEED SECRET #36

### Be assertive, not aggressive.

*Bravery isn't hard to find.*
*Skill is something else again.*
*Drivers who have only courage*
*don't last for long.*

**—Stirling Moss**

Have you ever seen Michael Schumacher or Michael Jordan look out of control? Perhaps Schumacher was out of control when trying to hold Jacques Villeneuve behind him at the last race of the 1997 Formula One season—with the World Championship on the line. Was that an assertive move? Or was it a desperate, aggressive move? Our feeling is he resorted to aggressiveness. Even the best can make mistakes. (In case you missed it, Schumacher bounced off the track while trying to defend an assertive passing attack from Villeneuve, who went on to clinch the World Championship.)

We're sure you have heard the saying, "Nice guys finish last." Some people relate being nice to not being assertive, but that's not the case. You can be nice, and still be assertive. But we doubt you can be unassertive and finish first. Perhaps the saying should be, "Unassertive guys finish last."

*Fear is not a stupid thing. Winning is not a*
*question of courage, but of faith in oneself and*
*in the car. A car is like a creature that lives,*
*with its own emotions and its own heart.*
*You have to understand it and love it accordingly.*
*I knew many drivers more courageous than me.*
*They are dead now.*

**—Juan Manuel Fangio**

## Risk and Fear

No doubt about it, racing is a risky endeavor. If you really want to succeed, you will have to take risks, not only on the race track, but with career decisions as well.

Whether it is on the track or off, taking a calculated, planned risk and failing is better than not risking at all. Of course, the goal is not to fail. The point is, you had better plan to deal with the risks. As the saying goes, "If you fail to plan, you plan to fail."

Of course, calculating and planning risk is the key. It would be foolish to risk taking a corner at 80 miles per hour that you normally take at 70, just as it would to accept an offer to race for the Williams Formula One team in the next Grand Prix having just graduated from your first racing school. In either case, it is best to work your way up in calculated increments.

*If you believe it can happen to you, how can you possibly do the job properly? If you're never over eight-tenths or whatever, because you're thinking about a shunt, you're not going as quick as you can. And if you're not doing that, you're not a racing driver.*

**—Gilles Villeneuve**

Fear comes in many forms, good and bad—or more accurately, useful and useless. It can be the fear of physical injury resulting from a crash. That fear usually limits your speed. We prefer to look at that as self-preservation, though, which can be a good thing. In fact, the only thing that deters you from going over the limit and crashing at every corner is this so-called fear.

Fear and desire are usually the opposite sides of the same coin. Some drivers want to achieve something, but are too afraid of it not working out. They focus on the fear of failure, which is another form of fear—a result—rather than the desire of making it work. When faced with an ultrafast sweeping turn, or a difficult career decision, they think about what may happen if they made a mistake.

If you concentrate instead on the solution or the goal and your performance, rather than the problem or the result, fear of failure disappears. If you keep a clear

*You have to be hungry all the time. You can never be satisfied. A complacent driver is a retired driver.*

**—Rusty Wallace**

mental picture of what you want to achieve, your mind will find a way of making it happen.

The fear of failure produces tension, which dis-integrates your brain, slows reflexes, and generally hurts your performance level. Of course, that usually produces the result you feared most.

Keep in mind how valuable feedback and awareness are to learning and improving your performance. There is no such thing as failure, only the results of doing something. And those results are simply feedback, or corrections guiding you toward your objective. Failure is just a result you didn't want, one that you can learn from and help you improve your performance.

## Motivation

If you are not 100 percent motivated, it is doubtful you will perform consistently at 100 percent. Focus on what you truly enjoy or love about the sport. Motivation mostly comes from the love of what you're doing. As part of your regular mental imagery sessions, see yourself enjoying the art of driving, experiencing the thrill of racing, loving every second of it!

Something most racers do not have to worry too much about, because of the high costs of testing and racing, can actually help increase your motivation level: moderation. Taking a break from the sport, to the point where you miss it, may be just what the motivation doctor ordered.

Racing can be such an all-encompassing passion that many drivers spend practically 24 hours a day, seven days a week eating, breathing, and living the

*Desire! That's the one secret of every man's career.
Not education. Not being born
with hidden talents. Desire.*

**—Bobby Unser**

sport. If that is you, when you finally get behind the wheel of your race car, some of the passion and burning desire to drive may be gone.

Keep your racing in perspective and a balance in your life. Remember why you race. Do not take yourself, your career, your racing too seriously. Have fun. After all, that is why you started racing, wasn't it? You may have to remind yourself of that every now and then!

## INNER SPEED SECRET #37

### Think about what you love about racing.

Having said that, it is your level of commitment and desire—your burning desire—that will determine, more than anything else, how often you win and how far you go careerwise in professional racing (if that is your goal).

Much of your motivation comes from your expectations as to how you will do. If you believe you will not do well in an event, most likely your motivation to do what is necessary to maximize your performance will not be there. Of course, this leads to a self-fulfilling prophecy. You don't expect to do well, so you don't prepare, which leads to a poor performance, which leads to a poor result, which meets your expectations.

*Determination that just won't quit—that's what it takes.*

**—A. J. Foyt**

Again, this is why it is so important to focus on your performance, and not the result. There is never any reason you cannot perform at your maximum, so there should never be any reason to become de-motivated.

*Racing isn't all about birds in hot pants and jets flying in and out of circuits. It is about traveling vast distances to spend 10 hours strapped in the car during testing. It's about denying a beer when you want one. It's not all parties. It's about going to bed at 10 p.m. I don't want to sound a martyr, but nothing is for nothing.*

**—Alan Jones**

*What I have achieved has been through determination, single-mindedness and doggedness.*

**—Nigel Mansell**

Having goals or objectives prior to each session or race event can certainly affect your motivation. Having goals that are positive and achievable, but challenging and performance-related, gives you something to strive for, something to go after. Conversely, goals that are unrealistic or easily achieved will most likely discourage and de-motivate you.

*As a racing driver there are some things you have to go through, to cope with. Sometimes they are not human, yet you go through it and do them just because of the feelings that you get by driving, that you don't get in another profession. Some of the things are not pleasant, but in order to have some of the nice things, you have to face them.*

**—Ayrton Senna**

### Perseverance, Commitment, and Dedication

Did you know that Michael Jordan was originally told he wasn't good enough to play for his high-school varsity basketball team? Of course, we all know he didn't take that evaluation and walk away from the sport. Instead, he practiced every day until he made the team, and the rest is history. The point is that he persevered—he never gave up.

*Although I do not have the gift of the gab and am completely charmless, I just persevere. I never give up.*

**—Damon Hill**

Making it to the top in motor racing takes a tremendous amount of work, sacrifice, commitment, perseverance, and dedication. Don't ever fool yourself: No matter how much talent you have, you will never be a winner in the top levels of professional racing (F1, Indy/Champcar, NASCAR, Sports Car, etc.) without those elements.

If we had to pick just one thing that a person requires to make a professional career in auto racing, it would be perseverance. Bobby Rahal was once quoted as saying that it takes 10 percent talent and 90 percent perseverance to make it in racing. We agree.

During a race, never give up. No matter how far behind you are, no matter how hopeless it seems, if you keep pushing there is a chance your competition will have problems. Focus your mind on that possibility. If you haven't pushed hard—if you've given up—you may not be close enough to take advantage of others' problems.

Commitment and perseverance alone will not guarantee success, but without them you can guarantee you won't perform to your maximum. Sure, there have been many drivers who have made huge commitments, who have persevered, who have made the sacrifices, and who have not made it to the top. But we also know of no driver who has made it who hasn't made the commitment, who hasn't sacrificed and persevered.

## Preparation

People often talk about the natural talent of such athletes as Michael Schumacher, Michael Jordan, Wayne Gretzky, and Tiger Woods. If there is one thing all these great athletes have in common, it is how hard they have worked, how much they have practiced, and the amount of time and effort they put into preparing for their sport.

There is a true story about Ayrton Senna that is a great example of how true natural talent mostly comes from hard work. A couple of hours after winning his first Formula One Grand Prix in Portugal in 1985, Senna was seen driving around the track in a street car. Remember now, this was after he had just totally dominated the entire race with one of his magical performances in the rain. And what was he doing driving the track in a street car? Trying to figure out how he could have performed even better. That's commitment to being the best. That's preparation. That is what is often confused for natural talent.

Michael Jordan would often show up early prior to a game, well before his teammates arrived, and practice his three-point shot. If someone of Jordan's abilities knows the value of practice and preparation, shouldn't you?

Winners go way out of their way to ensure they have prepared in every way possible. That includes your diet, physical exercise program, mental training program, even planning travel to suit yourself, ensuring your clothing is appropriate for sponsor functions, proper public relations, and so on.

## INNER SPEED SECRET #38

### Preparation is not just one thing —it's everything.

Race driving is all about control and discipline. Most, if not all, of the all-time great drivers (Senna, Schumacher, Prost, Stewart, Mears, Andretti) controlled their lives and everything around them. Their attention to detail was paramount. Their commitment to looking after their driving equipment was a good example. We doubt you'll often find a world champion who doesn't like things to be organized, controlled, disciplined, and prepared.

*I like the competition better than the victory, the fighting better than the winning.*

**—Stirling Moss**

*Racers are always looking for the quick and easy way to win. They're looking for the magic spring or the secret camshaft. Those things might exist, but I couldn't begin to tell you where to go and find them. If those things do exist, they won't make you a consistent winner. The people who win consistently aren't wasting their time looking for those things; they spend their time refining the basics and making sure they are prepared.*

**—Ray Evernham**

## Winning

We've talked a lot in this chapter about removing the emphasis or focus from winning and placing it strictly on the act of driving—on your performance; and how, by doing this, you will increase your chances of winning. So, does this mean that winning is not important? Of course it is! It matters very much. That is what racing is all about.

The objective of racing is to win, but the purpose of racing is to race.

Winning races is the objective of the sport, but it should not be the focus. Winning is the ultimate result of a great performance. A losing, but great performance has a more deep and long-lasting personal satisfaction level than a winning, but crummy performance. Use the strategies presented throughout this book to ensure you have great performances, rather than crummy ones. Do that and winning will look after itself.

*I am addicted to winning. I can't do without it. The more I win the more I want it.*

**—Ayrton Senna**

Of all the drivers we have worked with through the years, the ones who have the absolute burning desire—a need—to win, seem to have the knack of performing at their very best on a consistent basis. They are the ones who would do whatever it took to win. They spent the time preparing, physically and mentally. And they did win—more often than anyone else. But their focus always seemed to be on improving their own performance—the winning just looked after itself.

*Winning is what I expect to do. That is my baseline, my starting point. I don't get too emotional about winning; that is what I go motor racing for.*

**—Ron Dennis**

Some of the drivers we have worked with did not take losing very well, to put it mildly. Unfortunately, this attitude often led to more poor performances, and more losses. When discussing how upset they became after a loss, they would all claim it was because they were so competitive—they hated to lose. We don't know of anyone in racing who enjoys losing. But, the drivers who look at a loss as something to learn from—and no, not something to enjoy or be satisfied with—are the ones who most often came back to win next time out.

Competitive people—people who want or need to win—are the ones who most need to learn from their losses. Every race you compete in will have more losers than winners—it's the nature of the sport. If you become overly upset and focused on a loss, and never learn from it, you are bound to lose again and again.

*Of course it is speed that wins races. But a champion will always win his races as slowly as he can. Driving perfection, not recklessness, wins races constantly.*

**—Jackie Stewart**

**Strategies**

In all your mental imagery, see yourself in and out of the race car relaxed and calm. See yourself focused on performing at your maximum, not particularly concerned with your competition. See yourself completely comfortable in your surroundings out of the car, and with the speed in the car. See yourself confident in your ability to perform, and that you belong at the front of the field—no matter what, you are "going to the front." See your ideal level of upness—not too psyched, intense, or energized, but not too laid back either. See yourself as assertive, and making smart racing decisions. See yourself racing for the pure love of it, fully motivated to do whatever it takes to perform well. See yourself fully prepared—you've eaten well, you've physically and mentally trained—you're ready. See yourself facing some adversity, but overcoming it by persevering, demonstrating your commitment to yourself and others. See yourself dealing with pressure, placed on you by others, by focusing on your performance and letting that take care of the results.

Program all these feelings, these attitudes, states of mind, beliefs—relaxed, but intense. Calm, but energized. Psyched up, but in control. Focused, but aware.

See, hear, and feel yourself performing better than you ever have. And notice the result—winning—something you want more than anything else in the world, but knowing it was your performance that produced the result.

Write down on a piece of paper what success in racing means to you. What do you want to achieve? How do you want to feel? For some drivers, becoming World Champion is the only objective. For others, it's to get paid to race cars, no matter what type or level. Others still only want to race for the pure enjoyment of it, and whether they race at the amateur club level or make it in professional racing does not matter.

Then write down why you want to achieve that level of success. Is it to make lots of money, have lots of fame, feel good about yourself, for the sense of accomplishment, to fulfill the dreams of a parent, for the thrill of controlling a car at speed, to beat other drivers, or because you haven't found anything else you are really good at?

The point is, the reason doesn't matter. One reason is not any better than another. The key is to know why for your own personal motivation. The more honest you are with yourself, the more effective this information will be to your motivation level. When you need that little pick-me-up, focus on your ideal levels of success and the reasons you want them to come to fruition.

As we mentioned, success, and feelings of success, leads to further success. Take some time to recall and write down at least three of the best performances of your life. These do not have to have anything to do with racing, or have resulted in a victory or high grade. They can be how you performed in school, in another sport, something you accomplished in a job, or about a relationship. Make note of how you felt before, during, and after these performances. Recall every detail you can about them. Relive them, and write them down. Then, go back and read them every now and then, or update them with new experiences.

# Chapter 20

# "One"

There is a take-out pizza restaurant named Zen Pizzeria. A man walks in to order a pizza and says to the person behind the counter, "Make me one with everything."

The Zen philosophy of oneness, or becoming one with the act of doing something, certainly applies to driving a race car. How many times have you heard a driver talk about being one with the car? Ayrton Senna used to speak of it more often than most; and it showed in his driving. At Monaco in 1988, he qualified on the pole 1.4 seconds quicker than his teammate, four-time World Champion, Alain Prost! This is how he described that magical qualifying lap:

> When I am competing against the watch and against other competitors, the feeling of expectation, of getting it done and doing the best and being the best, gives me a kind of power that, some moments when I am driving, actually detaches me completely from anything else as I am doing it—corner after corner, lap after lap. I can give you a true example I experienced and can relate it.
>
> Monte Carlo '88, the last qualifying session. I was already on pole and I was going faster and faster. One lap after the other, quicker and quicker and quicker. I was at one stage just on pole, then by half a second and then one second and I kept going. Suddenly I was nearly two seconds faster than anybody else, including my teammate with the same car. And I suddenly realized I was no longer driving the car consciously.
>
> I was kind of driving it by instinct, only I was in a different dimension. It was like I was in a tunnel. Not only the tunnel under the hotel but the whole circuit was a tunnel.
>
> I was just going and going, more and more and more and more. I was way over the limit but still able to find even more. Then suddenly something just kicked me. I kind of woke up and realized that I was in a different atmosphere than you normally are. My immediate reaction was to back off, slow down. I drove back slowly to the pits and I didn't want to go out any more that day. It frightened me because I realized I was well beyond my conscious understanding. It happens rarely but I keep these experiences very much alive in me because it is something that is important for self-preservation.

When you are one with the car, you are no longer consciously thinking about driving, nor are you thinking about not thinking about driving. You are just driving. In fact, as soon as you begin to think about how you are one with the car, you no longer are.

Have you ever driven down a long highway, or perhaps on a route you've driven many times before, and all of a sudden realized you don't know how you've gotten to where you are? You were completely unaware on a conscious level of the driving you had just done—you were on autopilot. In fact, your conscious mind may have been thinking about something entirely different than driving. That is similar to being one with the act of driving in that there is no conscious thought of what you are doing. The big difference, though, is that when you are one with race driving you are acutely aware of what you are doing and everything surrounding you.

When you are one with the car, it is as if you and your car are in slow motion, you are so relaxed and have so much time to think. Driving at the limit and racing your competitors is effortless, easy. You are calm, yet intense and assertive. You are not worried, or even thinking about your result—it is almost as if you know what the result will be. You are confident in your performance. You are totally in control, and feel you can do no wrong. You are able to predict what is going to happen all around you. You have only one thought in mind, your picture of the ideal performance—your goal. You are completely focused on the act of driving, yet aware of everything—the cars around you, track conditions, your technique, your speed and traction, the car's handling characteristics. You are totally absorbed, mentally and physically, in the act of racing. You are operating on an instinctive level. You are loving every second of it!

A few years ago, one of our students related that after he has been on the track, he imagines what it would feel like to be a group of rubber cells on his tires, and what the other cells would say to him. If this sounds a bit far out to you, perhaps you should realize that Albert Einstein literally experienced his theory of relativity as the result of visualizing that he was on the head of a proton in motion!

Becoming one with your race car is to become a part of the movement, a part of the energy. The real question is whether you can become one with your car even when your car is not handling very well. It may be easy to be one with the car when it is perfect, but what about when it is not competitive? Yes, you can.

In fact, becoming one with your race car is one way of describing everything we've discussed in this book. Oneness with your car is driving subconsciously, by a program, without trying, without thinking—it is just doing, just driving. Of course, you cannot try to become one with the car. It is something you just do.

It only happens, though, through the use of all of the strategies and Inner Speed Secrets presented in this book, and then relaxing, letting go, trusting yourself, and just letting it happen. It is the weaving together of the strategies like the threads of a fine cloth, to make something stronger—more complete—and more enjoyable.

# Appendix A

# Personal Performance Program

A s we mentioned in the Introduction, the information in this book is only effective if you use it. Using the following list of strategies, develop your own unique Personal Performance Program—a program to maximize your performance. This program should be performed on a regular basis, and especially just prior to an event or a specific test, practice, qualifying, or race session.

Your Personal Performance Program should be defined by what you consider to be your greatest priorities—these are the exercises that you will be doing every day. At some point, your priorities will change—your Personal Performance Program will have to change. We would suggest that the Lazy 8's, Focus Stretches, Centering, and Cross Crawls be mandatory for every driver, every day.

Like learning a physical skill, each of these mental strategies will take some time for you to see and feel the results. If you try one of the strategies, and it doesn't seem to help immediately, keep at it. Give it some time. If a runner physically trained for only a week prior to a marathon, and then performed poorly, was the training strategy ineffective? No, the runner just didn't give it time. The same thing applies to your mental training strategies.

Expect each of these strategies to work, because they will, but realize it may take some time. Some drivers' performance actually suffers prior to making the big gains. Understand that it is all part of the natural learning process.

When Ross first began to work with Ronn in 1991, and started using many of the strategies presented here, he felt his performance actually got worse for a little while. "The problem was that I was having to think too much about them. But after a couple of months of regular use—and ever since then—they really made a big, positive impact on my driving—and everything else in my life. The difference was I stopped thinking about them, and just did them. They are now just part of my everyday routine." Use these strategies for long-term results.

It is probably a good idea to not take on every strategy all at once. Don't overload yourself. First, choose the areas you feel you have the most to gain from, or the ones with which you are most comfortable. Then begin to add more when the timing feels right. Eventually, given time and consistent use, all of these strategies will feel totally natural—you will probably do them without really thinking about them. They will have become another set of mental programs.

Last, it may take some experimentation, and some fine-tuning to find the right program for you. Your program will be unique to you. What works for you may not work for someone else, and vice versa. The key is to keep at it, while making note of—being aware of—any changes.

## Personal Performance Program
**Strategy**                                          **Comments**

- Neck rolls

- Bracelets

- Brain buttons

- Thinking caps

- Sensory input session

- Sports vision therapy

- Focus stretches

- Peripheral stretches

- Layered listening

- Preplan wanted thoughts

- List your positive and negative beliefs

- Recall and mentally relive past successes

- Centering

- Cross crawls

- Balance buttons

- Hook-ups

- Nondominant hand lazy 8s

- Alpha-state relaxation

- Mental imagery sessions:

  -Develop trigger words

-Program R-1, R-2, R-3

-Program beliefs

-Program ideal state of mind

-Program techniques/skills

-Program race scenarios

- Diet

- Program breathing

- Power breathing

- Adapt and program appropriate personality

- Narrow/broad attention

- Multitasking attention

- Focused concentration

- Program key decisions

- Define and use your preferred learning style

- Mentally image a peak performance

- List your racing goals/objectives

- Recall three of your life's best performances

- Ask awareness-building questions

- Traction sensing sessions

- Lazy 8s

- Mentally image oneness

# *Inner Speed Secrets*

1. Focus on your performance, not the result.

2. The goal is to get 100 percent out of yourself.

3. Although your skill level may have physical limits, your mind's potential is limitless.

4. Quality output depends on quality input.

5. Practice is programming.

6. Drive the race car on automatic pilot—subconsciously.

7. Program your mind.

8. Practice relaxation.

9. Program your mind with actualization.

10. Use mental imagery to program your entire mental mind-set.

11. If you can't do something in your mind—in your mental imagery—you will never be able to do it physically.

12. Integrate to get in the flow.

13. The better your sensory input, the better your skills.

14. What you think about is what you get.

15. You cannot *not* think about something.

16. You can only do what you believe you can do.

17. Act like who, or the way, you want to be.

18. Recall the feelings of your past successes.

19. Adapt your personality to suit the situation.

20. Focus on what you want, not what you don't want.

21. Program your decisions.

22. Practice the right skills.

23. Your performance is limited by what you feed your mind and body.

24. Program your breathing.

25. Know and use your preferred learning style.

26. Be aware of what you are doing.

27. Ask yourself positive, awareness-building questions.

28. What you see is where you go.

29. Smooth is fast.

30. Practice, at all times, the way you want to race.

31. Physical exercise strengthens your mind.

32. Build a winning team by example—lead the way.

33. Focus on your performance, and the results will look after themselves.

34. Relax, use less effort, and just let it happen.

35. Replay your successes.

36. Be assertive, not aggressive.

37. Think about what you love about racing.

38. Preparation is not just one thing—it's everything.

# Appendix C

# Recommended Reading

Bentley, Ross. *Speed Secrets.* Osceola, WI: MBI Publishing Company, 1998.

D'Adamo, Dr. Peter J. *Eat Right for Your Type.* New York: G.P. Putnam's Sons, 1996.

Dennison, Paul E. and Gail E. Dennison. *Brain Gym, Teacher's Edition.* Ventura, CA: Edu-Kinesthetics, Inc., 1989.

Diamond, Harvey and Marilyn Diamond. *Fit for Life.* New York: Warner Books, 1987.

Dyer, Dr. Wayne. *You'll See It When You Believe It.* New York: Avon Books, 1989.

Gallwey, Timothy. *The Inner Game of Golf.* New York: Random House, 1998.

Gallwey, Timothy. *The Inner Game of Tennis.* New York: Bantam Book, 1978.

Gelb, Michael J. and Tony Buzan. *Lessons from the Art of Juggling.* New York: Harmony Books, 1994.

Haas, Dr. Robert. *Eat To Win.* Toronto, Canada: Penguin Books, 1985.

Hannaford, Carla. *Smart Moves.* Arlington, VA: Great Oceans Publishers, 1995.

Hannaford, Carla. *The Dominance Factor.* Arlington, VA: Great Oceans Publishers, 1997.

Huang, Chungliang Al and Jerry Lynch. *Thinking Body, Dancing Mind.* New York: Bantam Books, 1992.

Jackson, Susan A. and Mihaly Csikszentmihalyi. *Flow in Sports.* Champaign, IL: Human Kinetics, 1999.

Kaplan, Robert-Michael. *The Power Behind Your Eyes.* Rochester, VT: Healing Arts Press, 1995.

Markova, Dawna. *The Open Mind.* Berkeley, CA: Conari Press, 1996.

McCluggage, Denise. *The Centered Skier.* Waitsfield, VT: Tempest Books, 1977.

Ostrander, Sheila and Lynn Schroeder. *Super Learning.* New York: Dell Publishing, 1979.

Robbins, Anthony. *Unlimited Power.* New York: Ballantine Books, 1986.

Sears, Barry. *The Zone.* New York: Harper Collins Publishers, Inc., 1995.

Shoemaker, Fred with Pete Shoemaker. *Extraordinary Golf.* New York: Penguin

Putnam Inc., 1996.

Wise, Anna. *The High Performance Mind.* New York: Jeremy T. Archer/Putnam Book, 1997.

Zukav, Gary. *The Dancing Wu Li Masters.* New York: William Morrow & Co., 1979.

We would like to know how *Inner Speed Secrets* has made a difference to you. To do that, or for information on our seminars or personal coaching services, please contact us at the address below.

Inner Speed Secrets
3530 Austin Bluffs Parkway
Colorado Springs, Colorado 80918
Phone: 719-260-0999
Fax: 719-260-9676
E-mail: Ross at rbentley@dowco.com
Ronn at porsche4@earthlink.com
Visit us at: www.speed-secrets.com